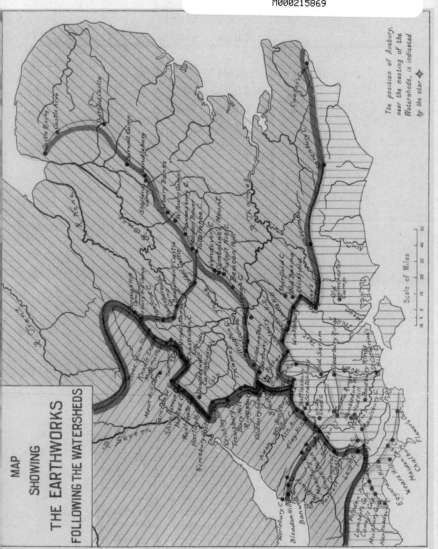

MAP

SHOWING

THE EARTHWORKS

FOLLOWING THE WATERSHEDS

The position of Avebury, near the meeting of the Watersheds, is indicated by the star ✦

Scale of Miles

First Published by
Methuen in 1914

This facsimile edition has been carefully scanned
and reprinted in the traditional manner by
THE LOST LIBRARY
5 High Street,
Glastonbury UK BA6 9DP

The LOST LIBRARY is a publishing house based in
Glastonbury, UK, dedicated to the reproduction
of important rare esoteric and scholarly texts for
the discerning reader.
Cataloguing Information
The Green Roads of England
R Hippisley Cox

ISBN 978 1 906621 05 6

Printed by Replika Press Pvt Ltd,
Haryana, India

**THE LOST
LIBRARY**

THE GREEN ROADS
OF ENGLAND

BY

R. HIPPISLEY COX

WITH 24 ILLUSTRATIONS BY W. W. COLLINS, R.I.
AND 8 MAPS IN COLOUR, AND 87 PLANS

PUBLISHED BY
THE LOST LIBRARY
GLASTONBURY, ENGLAND

First Published in 1914

" There is one road none may travel, but thou only "

TO

KOKORO

PREFACE

DURING the years I have lived among the Downs, and walked or ridden over many miles of their trackways, there has gradually grown up in my mind, a picture of the land at the time when these old trails were the only highways in the country.

Much is, and must be, guesswork, since all the evidence that remains to guide us, are the trackways and earthworks I have endeavoured to explain, and the best that can be attempted is to offer a theory that fits together the greatest number of facts.

The accepted explanation that the earthworks were tribal strongholds, used for local purposes only, appears to me impossible to maintain after examining a map of the watersheds. These hill forts are obviously arranged systematically along the watersheds, and there is much evidence to prove that they were connected together by a fully developed system of travel-ways.

In the south of England the common meeting-place of these hill roads was Avebury, where the greatest prehistoric monuments in Europe are still to be seen.   It is not unreasonable to suppose that this central gathering ground was the seat of government, and that its authority extended as far as the roads that radiate from it, and the earthworks that protected them.

The evidence, though mostly exclusive, points to the Stone Age as the period when the hill forts were built, and if the ridge roads can be attributed to the same time it follows that a civilization existed in this country long before the Celtic invasions.   To what stage that civilization had advanced it is difficult to realize, but the harbours connected with the ridge roads suggest that there was much trade over the seas, and the Stone Circles at Avebury, Stonehenge, Knowlton, and Rollright are proof that astronomy had advanced beyond the limits of savage outlook.   It is indeed not impossible that the men of the Bronze Age destroyed a civilization more fully developed than their own.   At least, the Sun worship of Neolithic man appears to have been a higher form of religion than demoniac Druidism.

My grateful acknowledgments are due to Mr W. W. Collins, R.I., for the attraction given to this book by his illustrations, to Miss Maud de Lacy

Lacy for her skilful preparation of the maps, and to Mrs Beresford Ryley for kindly revising the manuscript, and to the Ordnance Survey Department for the smaller plans of the camps.

It may be useful to my readers to know that I have found Bartholomew's coloured contour maps, $\frac{1}{2}$ inch to the mile, of great assistance in following the watersheds, and that the Ordnance Survey maps, one inch to the mile, are generally sufficient for tracing the smaller roads.

R. H. C.

OLDFIELD LODGE
    MAIDENHEAD.

CONTENTS

LIST OF ILLUSTRATIONS
IN THE TEXT

LIST OF MAPS IN COLOUR

THE GREEN ROADS
OF ENGLAND

CHAPTER I

AVEBURY

"There runs a road on Merrow Down."

THE triangular plateau of high land sur- **Ridge Roads** rounding the village of Avebury, in Wiltshire, forms the common meeting-place of the hills that divide the Upper Thames from the Severn, and from the small southern rivers. Before any drainage of the country had been attempted, all communication had of necessity to be made along these watersheds, the valleys being then little better than bogs and morass. In the down country, where agriculture has not destroyed them, these trackways may still be traced as broad green roads, showing evidences of ancient travel. Their turf, from long trampling, is finer and darker in colour than on the surrounding land. In their closer soil innumerable daisies turn the old trackways white during early summer, while here and there long lines of thistles mark the journeys of many pack-horses.

Pack Trails   The course of these green roads, in their ascent and descent of the hills, is frequently scored by pack-trails or ditches, still clearly to be seen, and commonly called " boundary mounds " on the maps.   They were formed originally by the hoofs of animals loosening the chalk, which was then quickly washed away by the rain.   In this way deep gullies were formed, broad at the top and narrowing at the bottom like the letter V.   When a trail had become disagreeably deep, another would naturally be commenced, until the hill-side was covered with ditches, radiating like the sticks of a fan from a point below.   In the course of ages, as the country became better drained, and wheeled traffic was introduced, it was found easier to keep to the level valleys.   Then the ancient ways along the hills were deserted and forgotten, and becoming covered with turf, have been preserved to us as we find them to-day.

Contour Forts   Along these trackways a system of contour forts follow the lines of hills from end to end, from Avebury to the English Channel, from Avebury to the Wash, and northwards, on the Cotswolds, to enclose the basin of the Upper Thames.   These forts are seldom more than a day's journey, or ten to twelve miles apart ; they are usually placed on the highest ground, following the contours of the land, and form more or less circular camps enclosing the hill-tops.   When protected with more than one tier of ramparts and ditches they are admirably placed for defence, but when surrounded by a single bank and ditch the position is usually less suggestive of defence, and it is not unlikely that such secondary camps served as cattle compounds to the larger fortresses. The camps are generally supposed to be of Neolithic origin, though from the strategic importance of their position they have doubtless been occupied by many succeeding waves of conquering races. Old Sarum is perhaps the best example of these hill forts and their history, as from its probable Neolithic origin, it is known to have been occupied by Celts, Saxons, Danes and Normans. Numerous hoards of flint instruments have been found within the area of most of the camps, but such finds are not positive proof of their dating to the Stone Age, as flints were in use for a long period after the introduction of bronze. The characteristic camp of the Bronze Age was, however, an irregular rectangular enclosure, placed on the slope of a hill, and it is almost certain that the circular forts belong to an earlier age.

On the spurs of the downs, and in the neighbour- Pit hood of the hill forts, are found groups of pit Dwellings dwellings, now hardly to be distinguished from small chalk-pits, but once the homes of Neolithic man. The favourite positions of these dwellings command wide and extensive views, wherever possible are placed on the sunny side of the hill, and they are supposed to have been roofed with sods or bracken. In the debris of their floors, among broken pieces of rough earthenware and charcoal, have been found the first proofs that domestic animals were used by our ancestors, the bones and teeth of dogs, sheep, pigs, oxen and horses being discovered, together with those of wolves and deer.

Dew-ponds   It was difficult to determine how the inhabitants of pit dwellings, and of the camps placed on the summits of the hills, were supplied with water, and such explanations as the higher level of the subsoil water, or the drying up of down streams, are hardly conclusive. The art of making dew-ponds has been known in the down country from the earliest times, and is practised to this day by special gangs of men, who have inherited their knowledge from tradition. In theory the art is simple enough. The chalk hills after absorbing the sun's heat by day, radiate it out at night, when the warmed air becomes loaded with moisture. If in a particular spot the radiation is checked by placing a non-conductor on the ground, the air is chilled as it passes over, and its moisture drops as dew. The usual method of making a dew-pond is to dig a shallow basin in the chalk, lay a layer of straw or rushes as a non-conductor, and puddle the surface with clay. As long as the rushes or straw remain dry, dew is deposited in hot weather to a considerable extent, and retained in the clay basin. The Biblical story of the moisture falling on Gideon's Fleece, whilst all the earth around remained dry, may be explained in a similar manner, but it is more difficult to account for the fleece remaining dry when the earth was wet. The accidental falling in of the roof of a pit dwelling, might easily have disclosed the possibilities of the dew-pond to Neolithic man, without his understanding the theory of its construction. Many shallow circular depressions, such as would be left by dried-up dew-ponds, are constantly met with in the neighbourhood of the camps and pit dwellings, and along the ridgeways they frequently occur at regular intervals. They must not, however, be mistaken for naturally formed Swallow Pits, which are larger, and most frequently found on the slopes of the hills.

The sarsen stones so common on the downs, **Sarsen** and frequently found collected in clusters or **Stones** circles at the most conspicuous points on the old travel-ways, are often called " Grey Wethers," from their being easily mistaken for sheep at a little distance. They are formed from the hardest parts of the loose sandstone that once covered the chalk, and that still exists at Bagshot, though on the downs it has long since been washed away. Great numbers have been removed, as at Avebury and Rollright, for building and road mending, and even recently it was proposed to make use of them in the construction of Southampton Docks.

Both long barrows and round barrows, especially

Tumuli the latter, are quite common objects of the wayside in the course of the green roads, and are often placed at the junction of a branch road, or on the conspicuous point of a hill, as if to serve as a guide or direction post.   Long barrows are mostly found singly, though Stukeley mentions fourteen as existing in his time at Avebury, of which only five now remain, and they are also numerous on the downs near Tilshead on Salisbury Plain.   In appearance they look like a bank of earth, measuring some sixty to a hundred yards long, with one end wider than the other, the broad end usually pointing to the east.   Within they are divided by sarsen stones into chambers placed on either side of a central passage.   Skeletons of a long-headed race have been found in these chambers, definitely proving these barrows to belong to the Stone Age. Round barrows occur both singly and in groups, the latter frequently arranged as if in deliberate relationship to each other, both as regards size and position, as on Overton Hill, Sugar Hill, and between Hackpen and Windmill Hill, such arrangements being possibly intended to give information to travellers according to an understood code of signals.   The round barrows or tumuli are simple mounds of earth varying greatly in size, sometimes surrounded by a ditch, and sometimes by a bank and ditch, the ditch being placed either within or without the bank.   The contents of the barrows depend chiefly upon their age ; in some cinerary urns are found, and these the British Museum authorities believe to be not older than 1000 B.C. In earlier barrows the burials are by simple inhumation, the primary interments being placed in the centre of the barrow below the ground level. In these older barrows finds of bronze are often associated with flint instruments, and both long and round skulls are found together. Again there are round barrows in which there are no signs of primary burials, and these are often the single barrows placed on conspicuous points along the trackways, where it is astonishing how well they are seen from many parts of the landscape. When first made their white chalk must have stood out still more clearly against the background.

The triangular tableland measuring some ten to **Avebury** twelve miles on either side, lying between the Pewsey Valley and the pastures of North Wilts, is the meeting-place of trackways from the Cotswolds, the Chilterns, Salisbury Plain and the Dorsetshire Hills. In its centre were erected Silbury, the largest artificial hill in Europe, and Avebury Temple, the largest stone circle in the world. Although they are the oldest existing monuments left by the inhabitants of our Island, we possess no earlier record of them than 1663 A.D., when Aubrey showed these wonderful works to His Majesty King Charles II., and by command wrote an account of their visit.

At the present day the Temple consists of a

The Temple circular earthen bank three-quarters of a mile in circumference, enclosing twenty-nine acres of level land. Immediately within the bank is a great ditch, originally thirty feet deep, but now averaging fifteen feet only, owing to the silting up of

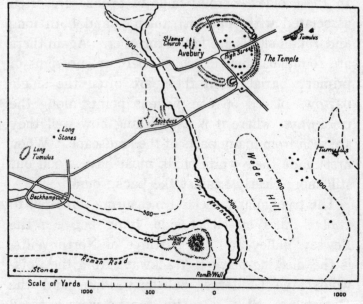

Silbury Hill and the Temple

many centuries. The bank stands fifteen feet above the ground level, or forty-five feet from the bottom of the original ditch. Skirting the inner margin of the ditch was a circle of large stones, of which Dr Stukeley says forty-four were standing in 1722, and that the sites of other stones to the number of a hundred could be traced. Within this large circle were two smaller double circles, of which the outer rings consisted of thirty stones, and each inner ring of twelve stones. In the centre of the Southern ring was a huge stone measuring twenty-seven feet high, and eight feet broad. In the centre of the Northern ring were three large stones, one of which fell in 1713 and measured twenty-one feet long, the middle stone was sixteen feet broad, and the third stone stood seventeen feet above the ground. Of all these circles only eighteen stones are now left.

Avebury

They are neither chiselled nor shaped as are the stones of Stonehenge, and from their signs of weathering are considered to be at least twice as old. The twenty-nine acres enclosed by the Temple are divided into unequal quarters by the crossing of the modern roads, which now forms the centre of the village. At the point where the roads issue from the Temple the bank has been thrown down and the ditch filled up, while a further portion of the bank near the Church has been removed. Many of the houses in the village are built with sarsen stones from the Temple, one

Tom Robinson in the eighteenth century being especially active in this work of destruction.   He

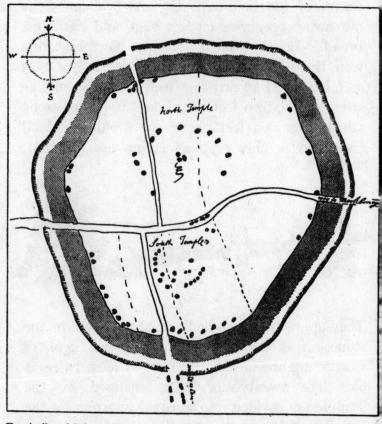

Facsimile of John Aubrey's Plan of the Great Earthwork, Foss within it (tinted), and Stones at Avebury in Wiltshire.   Taken about A.D. 1663.

From "Aubrey's Monumenta Britannica" MS. in the Bodleian Library.

first heated the stones and then soused them with cold water, when they were easily broken with sledge-hammers, and it is said that one stone alone yielded twenty good cartloads.

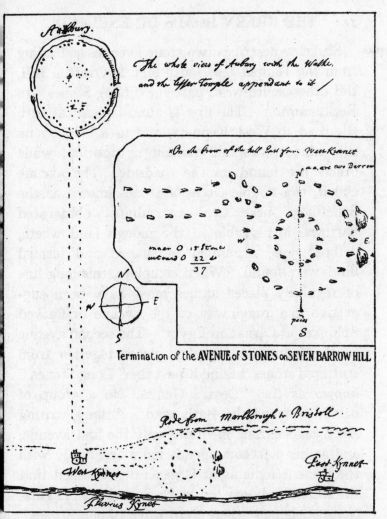

The whole view of Aubury with the Walke,
and the Upper Temple appendant to it

×On the brow of the hill East from West Kennet

a.a. are two Barrows

inner O 18 Stones
utward O 22 do
       37

Termination of the AVENUE of STONES on SEVEN BARROW HILL

Rode from Marlborough to Bristoll.

West Kynnet   East Kynnet

Fluvius Kynes

Facsimile of John Aubrey's General Plan of Avebury in Wiltshire, including
the Avenue of Stones leading to the Circles on Seven Barrow (now
Overton) Hill. Taken about A.D. 1663.

From " Aubrey's Monumenta Britannica" MS. in the Bodleian Library.

Avenue   Stukeley describes two stone avenues as leading from the Temple, one south-east to Overton Hill, the other south-west, past the "Long Stones" to Beckhampton. The first is almost identical with the road to West Kennett, and in a field by its side nine stones still remain in position, while others are found on the roadside. The avenue ended in a double circle of stones known as the Sanctuary, near two now almost obliterated barrows, just visible in the plough land where, Aubrey says, a number of shaped and formed flints were found. When complete, this long line of regularly placed stones must have been suggestive in a rough way of the Avenue of Carved Sphinxes at Carnac in Egypt. The second avenue to Beckhampton, Stukeley pieces together from scattered stones, taking it past the "Long Stones" known as the "Devil's Quoits," to a group of barrows beyond the Bath road. Aubrey, writing sixty years earlier, mentions only the first avenue, and as his plan corresponds more accurately with the present remains, it is generally assumed that the second only existed in Dr Stukeley's imagination. Originally there were three "Long Stones" or "Devil's Quoits," recalling the Bride, the Bridegroom and the Parson at Stanton Drew, but one of these stones was destroyed by the villagers, when it is said a large "fossil skeleton" was found, though of what kind is not stated.

From the Temple, Silbury Hill can just be seen

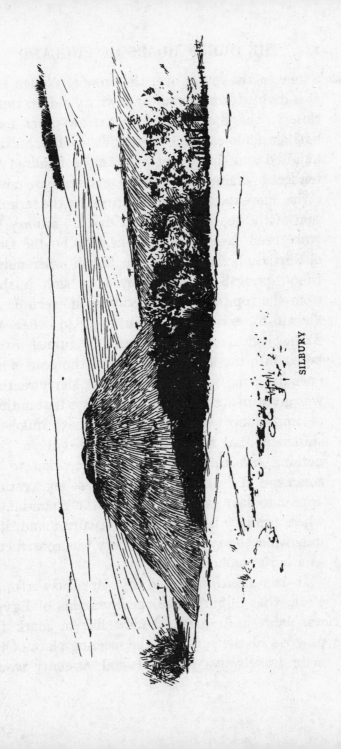

SILBURY

Silbury Hill a mile to the south, over the brow of Waden Hill. It is divided from a spur of down by a deep trench close to the Bath road, two narrow paths being left, as if for carrying up the soil. The hill is a hundred and thirty feet high, and a hundred and ten feet in diameter at the top, and the base covers rather more than five acres, formed by the termination of the separated spur of down. Silbury has twice been excavated, once in 1777 by the Duke of Northumberland and Colonel Drax, when miners from Cornwall were employed to sink a shaft from the top, of which operations no records are known to exist, and again in 1849 when the Archæological Institute caused a tunnel to be bored into the hill from the west, the scar of the opening being still visible. Dean Merryweather, who gives an account of the work, says that nothing of importance was found, and that Stukeley's statement that a monarch was buried there " has nothing but the pleasures of conception to re-commend it." As neither of these excavations appear to have penetrated below the ground level, where primary interments are usually found, it is impossible to say whether Silbury was constructed as a burial mound or not.

It has been suggested by Mr Cotsworth, of York, that Silbury, like the Pyramids of Egypt, was built as a great shadow hill to mark the progress of the sun. As the meeting-place of the main travel-ways of the Island, Avebury would be an appropriate centre for the erection of a national Sun Temple and Shadow Hill, from which to issue edicts as to the proper seasons for seed-time and harvest. Man in the nomadic and pastoral stage, as in early Biblical days, measured time by the moon, but when he adopted agriculture and became dependent on the seasons, it would have been more convenient for him to reckon the progress of the year by the sun. To ascertain the exact length of the year, 365.242 days, was a matter of great difficulty, requiring many centuries of thought and experiment, for if the quarter day is not taken into account, the calendar in a hundred years becomes inaccurate to the extent of 25 days. The length of the year once established, and divided into months, weeks and days, it was possible to mark the divisions of time by the appearance and disappearance of the stars, when the use of the shadow hill would be discontinued, and its purpose in the course of ages forgotten. The shadow of a pole placed on the top of Silbury falls to the north on the level meadows of the Kennett, the daily gauge being about four feet, or almost exactly that of the Great Pyramid.

The open spaces surrounding these two great monuments are crowded with the works of Neolithic man, and of the Celts who succeeded him. It is hardly accurate any longer to speak of them as " Prehistoric," for the men who lie buried in the chambered barrows and tumuli on the downs have left evidences of their lives, beliefs and doings, almost as full as the written documents of a later day. Settling in the land some time between 10,000 B.C., the date of the last glacial period, and the introduction of Bronze about 2000 B.C., they accomplished as much as modern men with similar limited means could do to-day. Their brain pans were as large as those of the modern European ; they worshipped the sun, studied the heavens, believed in a life after death, and intellectually appear to have been superior to the race that succeeded them and introduced demoniacal druidism. They not only knew the use of fire and boiling water, domesticated their animals, and grew grain, but from the evidences of their fortresses seem to have preserved peace and exercised a wide authority over the land.

The Plains of Avebury appear to have been the centre of their government. It was the meeting-place of all their highways, and although much has been destroyed, nowhere else are the evidences of their handwork so numerous.

The road leaving the village by the east soon becomes a field-path, and beyond the Temple passes a small square camp with a tumulus close to the rampart. Above on the slopes of Overton Hill are seen the low banks of an irregular square camp of the Bronze Age. A line of tumuli extends across the lower ground to Windmill Hill, on the brow of the hill is a long barrow near a chain of eight tall tumuli covered with trees, and close by are numerous collections of sarsen stones.

These groups of sarsen stones mark the course of the Great Ridgeway, where its southern and western branches unite to continue their joint course over Hackpen Hill to Barbury Camp, giving off a branch near Old Totterdown, that

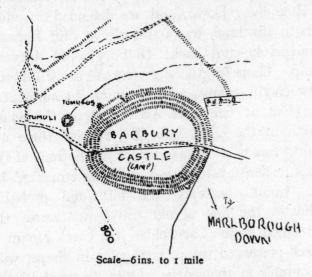

Scale—6 ins. to 1 mile

leads to a large collection of sarsen stones, and a cromlech known as the Devil's Den, in Clatford Bottom.

Barbury stands at the head of the Og Valley on the northern point of the Avebury triangle, and is defended by a double line of banks and ditches, while surrounding it are evidences of extensive early settlements. At the foot of the hill there are tumuli and numerous pack-trails

Barbury Camp

2

that point to communication with Bincknol Camp, three miles away, overlooking the watershed of the Thames and the Avon. This camp stands on the edge of the first escarpment of the chalk, as it rises from the level pastures of North Wilts, and has suffered much from the falling away of the cliff. These cliffs extend south for ten miles to Roundway Down, and are defended, in addition to Bincknol, by earthworks at Cliff Pypard, Bradenstoke-cum-Clack, Oldbury, and Oliver's Camp. Short lengths of green road are still found between the camps, as if continuous communication had at one time existed along the whole length of the cliffs. At Cliff Pypard there are slight remains of an earthwork at the foot of the chalk, where a steep and deep trail marked by two tumuli descends the hill, and probably indicates the line of old travel-way across the watershed to the Cotswolds. On Clack Mount is a well-preserved camp, triangular in shape, with a tumulus in the centre. Close by are the interesting remains of Bradenstoke Abbey and Tithe Barn.

Oldbury Camp

Beyond the Bath road two tumuli stand on the ascent to Oldbury Camp, the position being clearly marked for many miles round by the Lansdowne Monument, stated to have been erected in commemoration of the birth of King Edward VII. The fortress is strongly defended by double banks and ditches. Below it a white horse

was cut in the chalk in the year 1780, and is considered the best specimen of its species in Wiltshire.
A long ridge of down carrying a line of tumuli
towards Beckhampton shows the direction taken
by the old coach road to Bath. Morgan's Hill

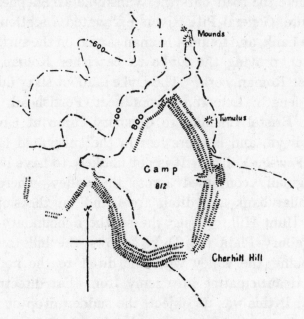

Scale—1 in. to 300 yards

Oldbury Camp

and King's Play Hill, wonderfully worked into
lynchetts, lead to Roundway Down, where a curious
little earthwork known as Oliver's Camp stands
on the edge of a steep cliff, and towards the down
is defended by a bank and ditch. Roundway is
scattered over with many tumuli, and it was

here that Charles' army defeated Fairfax before marching to its own defeat at Newbury.

The road from Beckhampton to Devizes passes through the middle of the Avebury triangle, the downs on either side being thick with tumuli. Where the road cuts the Wansdyke at Shepherds Shore, General Pitt Rivers excavated a section of the bank, and found a Roman sandal on the surface level, proving the Dyke to be either Roman or Post-Roman work. The Dyke is about sixty miles in length, extending from near Portishead, on the Bristol Channel, to Chisbury Camp at Great Bedwyn, and is there lost in the cultivated land of Pewsey Valley. It is not unlikely to have been originally continued across the valley, where a similar bank and ditch are found on the slopes of Ham Hill. Along the southern boundary of Avebury Plain the Dyke follows the hills overlooking the valley with the ditch to the north, as if anticipating an enemy from that direction. But if this was its object, the sudden drop of the hills immediately in the rear does not suggest a well-selected line of defence.

On the hills overlooking Pewsey Valley there are small camps at Rybury and Knap Hill, and on the side of Walker's Hill a poor specimen of a white horse was cut in 1812. The lower spur of the hill carries a long barrow known as the Giant's Grave, with an unusually narrow and sharp ridge. Martinsell Hill, terminating the eastern corner of the triangle, is the site of a complete Neolithic settlement, including dew-ponds, a cattle compound, pit dwellings, a flint quarry, lynchetts, ditches of defence, and deep cattle tracks formed by much going and coming of beasts from the valley.

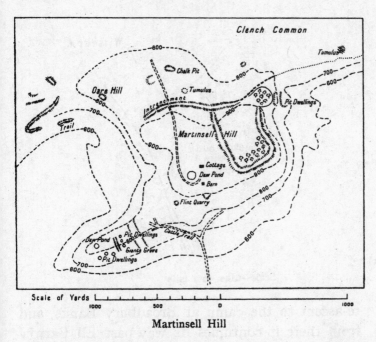

Martinsell Hill

Near the groups of sarsen stones on Overton Hill, on the high ground overlooking the Temple, the Ridgeway, as has been seen, divides into its southern and western branches. The southern or Salisbury Plain branch crosses the Bath road near seven large barrows, arranged in a manner suggesting design rather than accident,

The Ridgeway

and indicating perhaps some meaning to ancient travellers. After passing the river at East Kennett, the trail follows the downs to Walker's Hill, and descending below the Giant's Grave, becomes lost in Pewsey Valley. There are, however, trails on the Southern Hills indicating its

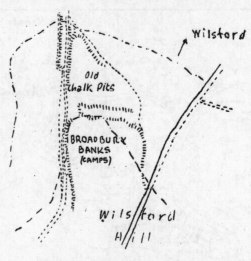

Scale—6 ins. to 1 mile

re-ascent to the camp at Broadbury Banks, and from there it continues its way past Ell Barrow to Stonehenge and Old Sarum.

The western branch of the Ridgeway, also commencing on Overton Hill, follows the line of eight round tumuli and one long barrow along the summit of the hill, and then crosses the river at West Kennett. The trail mounts the downs close to the Long Barrow, now in the care of the

National Trust, and can be traced by a succession
of dew-ponds to the back of St Ann's Hill. Across
the watershed of the Somersetshire and Wiltshire
Avons, its course may perhaps be indicated by a
green road, named the Lydd Way, that leads to
the high ground above the village of Urchfont.
Near the tumulus at this point the Ridgeway
joins the green road from Inkpen Beacon, and
then continues its journey westward along the
edge of the chalk, as far as the mouth of the Axe
in Devonshire.

CHAPTER II

THE RIDGEWAY FROM SALISBURY PLAIN
TO THE MENDIPS

" Afoot and light-hearted I take to the open road."

ALONG the northern edge of Salisbury Plain, overlooking Pewsey Valley, the green road from Inkpen and Fosbury passes Casterley Camp and Broadbury Banks, and near the tumulus above Urchfont joins the main Ridgeway. From here the road runs as a single trail to St John of Gores, arriving at the tumulus on Lavington Down, where it turns to the right over Littledown to Coulston Hill, and passes the long barrow above Tinhead village. Beyond Edington it leaves some terracings at the top of the cliff, and finally reaches Bratton Castle. From Lavington Down, what is now a better-marked trail, runs to Imber and Warminster, making a short cut to the head of the Wylye Valley. Nevertheless the trail to Bratton Castle has the better claim to be considered the Ridgeway, for throughout its length from the Thames at Streatley it has kept to the edge of the chalk, linking up the chain of great fortresses that keep watch over the country to the north.

Bratton Castle is one of the most imposing and commanding earthworks on the whole line of the Ridgeway. It occupies the summit of a steep hill above Westbury, encloses twenty-three acres, while the outer rampart measures just short of a mile, and is defended by triple ditches near the

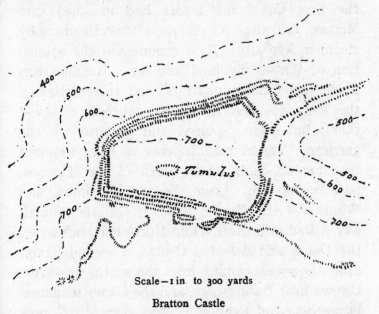

Scale—1 in. to 300 yards

Bratton Castle

entrance facing the downs. Within, on the left, is a long barrow, but as the interior has at various times been under tillage, other remains of early occupation have been destroyed, though flint instruments and Roman coins have frequently been discovered. On the slope of the hill below the western end of the camp an ancient white horse is cut in the chalk, but unfortunately has been modernized, and given the improved outlines due to the introduction of Arab blood.

It was on the downs and in the valley round Edington that Alfred, after nine years' fighting, brought his arduous campaign against the Danes to a successful issue in the year 879 A.D. From the East Coast the Danes had marched into Mercia, and after its conquest took Reading by storm in 871 A.D. Then commenced the subjection of Wessex by land and sea ; Reading was made their winter quarters, and there Ethelred the Unready, and Alfred his brother, attacked them, but were repulsed and pursued by the garrison. The retreat appears to have followed the line of chalk cliffs south of the Thames, past Perborough, Aston Terryl, Letcombe, and Wantage, Alfred's birthplace. On the fourth day Alfred rallied on White Horse Hill, turned on the Danes and defeated them. A second Saxon army, however, coming from the south, was overthrown near Basingstoke, and the Danes remained in possession of Reading. Next year, Alfred, now being king, attacked the Danes at Wilton, and though both sides claimed the victory, the Danes agreed to withdraw from all parts of Wessex, including Reading. There followed four years of peace, which appears to have been broken by Alfred capturing six of the enemy's ships. The Danes retaliated the following year by taking the seaport of Wareham, and for the next three years

practically over-ran the whole of Wessex from
Reading to Exeter. It was during this period
that Alfred sought refuge in the Isle of Athelney,
amid the swamps of Somersetshire, where the incident of the burnt cakes took place. In 897 A.D.
whilst the Danish force was lying at Edington

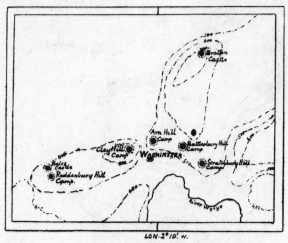

Scale—¼ in. to 300 yards

Warminster District

in apparent security, Alfred quietly collected an
army at Brixton Deverill, not twelve miles away,
and making a night march to Cley Hill, commenced
his attack next morning. The Danes took refuge
in their defences—possibly Bratton Castle—but
surrendered after fourteen days' siege, when the
whole invading army became Alfred's prisoners.
It was not Alfred's business to free England from
the Danes, indeed his resources could hardly have

been sufficient to make the attempt, and as
they were to be his neighbours for the future, he
came to a friendly understanding with them, per-
suaded them to become Christians, and after enter-

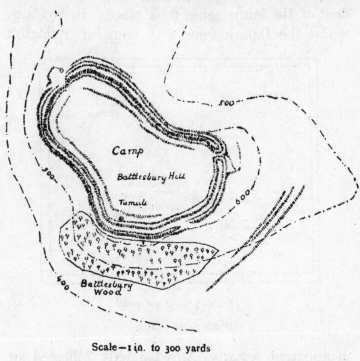

Scale—1 in. to 300 yards

Battlesbury

taining them royally at Wedmore, arranged for
their departure from his own kingdom of Wessex.
Best precaution of all, he commenced building the
British Navy, always the right defence for an
Island, and the only possible one when the popula-
tion depends for its food from over the seas.

The spurs of hill enclosing the watershed that

BATTLESBURY AND SCRATCHBURY CAMPS

divides the Wylye Valley from the sources of the
Frome, are fortified by a cluster of ancient earthworks greater in number than on any area of
Battlesbury a similar size in the Kingdom. The imposing
fortress of Battlesbury appears to have been the
centre of the defence. It encloses twenty-three
acres, is inaccessible on the west and north-east
owing to the steepness of the hills, and is defended
by as many as four ramparts where approached
from the down. In the south-west corner there
are three tumuli occupying the inner ditch and
rampart, and the hill-side outside the camp on the
east has been cut into lynchetts, some of which
have been smoothed away by modern ploughing.
Scratchbury The neighbouring hill to the south is named
Camp Middle Hill, and has three tumuli near the summit.
Beyond, not a mile and a half from Battlesbury, is
Scratchbury Camp, surrounded by a single bank
and ditch, enclosing forty acres, and containing
seven barrows, one a very large one in the south-
west corner. There is also a long barrow beyond
the hill to the south-east, and a group of tumuli
on the next hill above Norton Bavant.

The slopes of the little valley that separate
these camps from the downs are terraced in many
places, while on its eastern side are numerous
tumuli, including a long barrow facing Middle
Hill. A ditch from Bratton Castle follows the
drove road from Bowls Barrow to Yarnbury. At
the head of the valley, hardly a mile north of

Battlesbury, is an unnamed earthwork of considerable size, enclosed by a single bank and ditch, and containing a long barrow on its highest point.

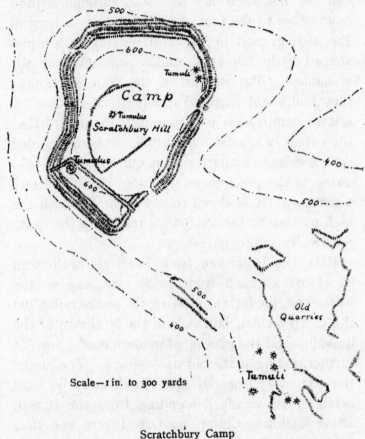

Scale—1 in. to 300 yards

Scratchbury Camp

A ridge from Warminster Down stretches west for two miles to Arn Hill, where the remains of an old camp can still be traced, though much mutilated by the working of limekilns and chalk-pits. The spur of down is further protected by a transverse ditch of defence.

Cley Hill Camp

The continuation of the outer edge of the chalk can be traced from Arn Hill through Upton Scudamore to the foot of Cley Hill, an offshoot of the high ground to the west, ending in a cone-shaped little hill that stands sentinel over the watershed. The summit of the main portion of Cley Hill, eight hundred feet high, is enclosed by a large camp, with two tumuli in the centre that show sharply against the skyline. It is surrounded by a foss and rampart, and is quite inaccessible—owing to the precipitous slopes of the hill. Only a narrow ridge of down connects the hill with the high plateau to the west, thus rendering the camp practically impregnable.

Both the Ridgeway from Bratton Castle, and its shorter branch from Imber, descend to the watershed, the latter following the pack-trails from the camp on Arn Hill, where the workings of the limekilns and the making of modern roads, prevent further tracing of the old travel-ways. The line of the Ridgeway from Bratton Castle may be indicated by the trails descending from the tumuli above Galloway Clump, on Cow Down, and that point in the direction of a tumulus standing in the orchard of Temple Farm at Scudamore. From the village a drove road follows the four hundred foot contour to Norridge Common, and continues as a disused green road to the foot of Cley Hill.

Beyond Cley Hill it is a matter of inference that the Ridgeway follows the edge of the chalk hills, for here alas, the green turf ends, the downs have been destroyed, and the country enclosed, and it is not possible that the old trackways should have been preserved, though many lengths

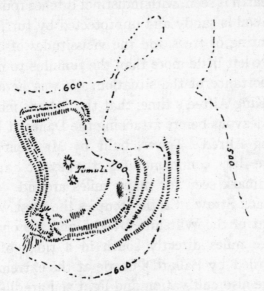

Scale—1 in to 300 yards

Cley Hill, Camp

of modern road occupy the positions where the Ridgeway might be expected. Roddenbury Castle stands on the cliffs three miles from Cley Hill, with a small earthwork named Hayes Castle just outside its banks. Six miles further, on King's Settle Hill, Jack Straw's Castle occupies a site that must have been a great gathering place in ancient times.

Jack Straw's
Castle

2

It was in this neighbourhood that the road from Sarum to the Mendips crossed the Ridgeway, and that the Ridgeway divided into the two branches leading to Shaftesbury and Camelot. Of Jack Straw's Castle practically nothing remains. In the wood at the edge of the hill only a small mound of earth is seen, with indistinct ditches round it, for the soil is sandy and unprotected by turf, and the planting of trees and the vicissitudes of centuries have left little more than the tumulus to mark the importance of the situation. It was here, as late as King Alfred's time, that the Saxons made their rendezvous before attacking the Danes at Bratton. King Alfred's Tower, built by Mr Henry Hoare close by, commemorates the event, and is a landmark seen for many miles around.

Jack Straw's Castle occupies the most westernly point of the Wiltshire Downs, and the chalk ends three miles directly south in a ridge of gravel, guarded by Ballard's Castle at the extreme point. Here also cultivation and light soil are ill-adapted for the preservation of earthworks, and now little remains of Ballard's Castle but a few indistinct banks enclosing a space of about an acre.

What may be the origin of the name " Jack Straw " has not been explained, but it is probably more than a coincidence that the public house on Hampstead Heath known as " Jack Straw's Castle," should also occupy the site of an ancient earthwork.

At the head of the valley to the east of Jack
Straw's, the Stour rises at Six Springs, in the
beautiful grounds of Stourhead, once the seat of
Sir Richard Colt Hoare.   As the river runs through
the village of Penselwood, the rocky ground on

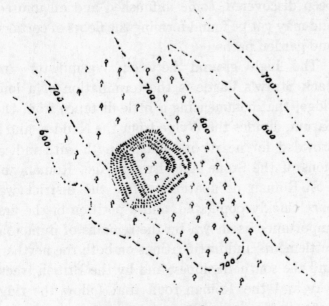

Scale—1 in. to 300 yards

Camp near Jack Straw's Castle

either side, extending to over seven hundred acres,
is excavated into numberless holes known as the
" Pen Pits," the pits measuring as much as fourteen
feet in depth and from seven to thirty feet in
diameter.   The Pen Pits have given rise to much
controversy, and were thought at one time to be
the site of a British Metropolis, but General Pitt

Rivers has shown conclusively that they were old quarries, from which the stone was obtained for making querns, or handmills for grinding corn. These quarries must once have been a thriving industry, for immense numbers of querns have been discovered, some unfinished and all unused, and may yet be found forming the floors of cottages and garden paths.

Between the Wylye and the Nadder   The high ground between Warminster and Jack Straw's Castle is the termination of a long ridge, that commencing a little distance from Old Sarum, divides the Wylye from the Nadder, and is crowded for nearly its whole length with indications of the Stone Age, Bronze Age, Roman and Post-Roman occupation. That the district was once thickly populated, and a position of the first importance, is shown by the remains of numerous settlements and fortifications on both the northern and the southern slopes, and by the British trackway and the Roman road that follow the ridge between the two rivers.

The Roman road, starting from Old Sarum, is accompanied by a ditch on its south side, which, after crossing the Wylye, is continued along the southern front of the hill to Ham Hill Ditches, where it is strengthened by two additional rows of ramparts. There are indistinct traces of occupation beyond the ditches to the south of Groveley Wood, while further on Wick Ball Camp standing above the village of Dinton, with a single ditch and bank measuring thirty feet high, encloses an area of about nine acres. The spurs of the hill on the northern slopes of the Down overlooking the Wylye, are nearly all occupied by ancient earthworks. Above Stapleford, Groveley earthwork consists of an entrenchment a mile in length, strengthened in the centre by three lines of strong ramparts, and protected a British village that once covered a space of about sixty acres. Many packtrails ascend the hill from the direction of Stapleford, where a little earthwork close to the ford marks the junction of trackways from Stonehenge, Bratton and Yarnbury.

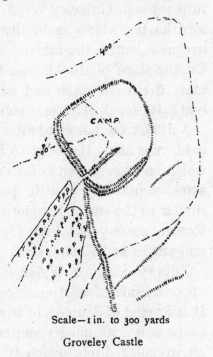

Scale—1 in. to 300 yards

Groveley Castle

Groveley Castle commands the point of the next hill. Oddly enough the work has been left unfinished on the northern side, and Colt Hoare, after examining the ground, found no signs of occupation. This work lies directly south-west of Stonehenge, in a straight line with Sidbury Camp to the north-east, but whether by accident or design no one can say. On the opposite spur of down are many tumuli, and an earthwork about two hundred yards in circumference, with a tumulus in the centre. Behind these works the Roman road runs through Groveley Wood, emerging at Langford Castle, where again there is a collection of irregular banks, the remains of a British village. On the slope of the hill can be traced a slightly marked circular ditch and bank, while numerous lynchetts speak of ancient cultivation.

A ditch from Langford after crossing the Roman road, runs along the ridge to Stockton earthwork, which encloses the site of a village of about sixty acres, containing a little pentagonal earthwork similar to the one at Langford. Much British and Roman pottery has been found here, as well as mill-stones and Roman coins.

Bilbury Ring or Wylye Camp stands on the opposite side of a steep coombe from Stockton. It is formed of double and triple banks, circular in shape and containing seventeen acres. Within is an irregular ditch, which it has been suggested was once connected with Stockton, and which is considered to be of earlier date than the ramparts.

On the succeeding spurs of down, as far as Warminster, are many lynchetts and tumuli, and these were even more numerous before the enclosure of the commons. Beyond Corton Long Barrow on White Hill is an unusual little earthwork shaped like the letter D, an acre and a half in size, and on the far side of the same hill, by the trail from Tytherington, are evident remains of a British village. On the north side of the road from Heytesbury to Maiden Bradley are three small earthworks. The first of these, connected to the road by a causeway, consists of an oval bank with a ditch on the inside, and encloses about half an acre of level turf, which may have served originally as a small amphitheatre. In an adjoining wood is a square Roman camp, about three-quarters of an acre in extent, known as " Robin Hood's Bower," and on Sutton Common are the indistinct remains of another small earthwork.

From Stockton the Roman road is carried through Great Ridge Wood, where it is lost. It appears to have been continued along the line of road from Monkton Deverell to Maiden Bradley, making for the watershed between the river Brue and the Frome, and is found again in the same straight line near Witham Friary at the foot of the Mendips. From Monkton Deverell the more ancient track-way—which has taken nearly the same line as the Roman road—is represented by two trails, one following Brimsdown Hill and the second keeping along the ridge of Rodmead Hill. Enclosed by these two lines of hills is a long narrow ridge called the Knoll, with a tumulus at the furthest end, nine hundred and forty-five feet above the sea level, which marks the highest point

in Wiltshire.   South of the Knoll, in the Deverell
Valley, the Wylye has its source at Bratchwell
Spring near Kilmington, the name of the valley
" Dive Rill " being given it from the stream dis-
appearing underground during Summer.   Brims-

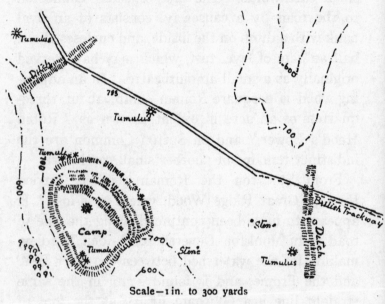

Scale—1 in. to 300 yards

Whitesheet Castle

down Hill, with its spurs Bidcombe Hill and
Cold Kitchen Hill, is covered with many tumuli,
ditches and excavations, and the green road
along its summit appears to be making for the
Mendips in the same direction as the Roman road.
Rodmead Hill, bordering the Deverell Valley to
the south, is also crowded with a number of tumuli,
Flint Barrow being specially conspicuous on the

point of down above Kingston Deverell, while the trackway along the ridge passes two more small earthworks on its way to Whitesheet Castle. **Whitesheet Castle** This camp is of considerable strength, defended by a single rampart where it overlooks the valley, but fortified by three banks and ditches towards the downs on the north. It is irregularly circular in form, with a mound in the centre. There are numerous tumuli and ditches on the surrounding downs, where the trail from Jack Straw's Castle can be clearly seen.

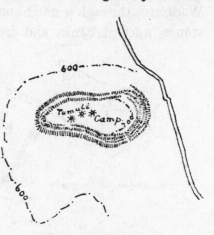

Scale—1 in. to 300 yards

Small Down

Beyond the little valley to the west of Jack Straw's Castle, the Mendip Hills stretch across the Plains of Somerset **The Mendips** to the Bristol Channel, continuing the long line of high ground that runs east and west the whole width of England, from Dover to Winchester, from Winchester to Old Sarum, and from Old Sarum to the Mendips. From Brimsdown Hill the trail probably crossed to the Mendips by the watershed of the Brue and Frome, and made its ascent to Beacon Hill by Small Down Camp

above Evercreech, following much the same line
that was taken in later times by the Romans,
only that they placed their camp at Leighton near
Cranmore.

It appears that there was also a route to the
Mendips from Bratton Castle, that running north
of Frome passed the great camps of Tedbury and
Wadbury, through a neighbourhood rich in sarsen
stones, ancient banks and cromlechs.

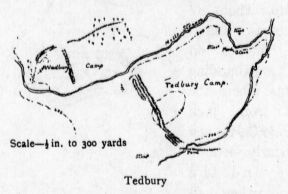

Scale—⅛ in. to 300 yards

Tedbury

Beacon Hill   In the loose earth of Beacon Hill the ditch and
bank of a circular earthwork can still be made
out, surrounded in its immediate neighbourhood
by many tumuli. At all times the site with its
wide outlook must have been of importance, and
it was here that the Foss Way, running north,
crossed the Roman road to the west, making
a meeting-place for Romans from all parts of
the Island. The green plains of Somersetshire
are spread out below, with Wells, Glastonbury,
Avalon and Athelney in their folds. It is the

cradle of the Anglo-Saxon race, where Alfred prepared his victories and Arthur lies buried. In Jerusalem only was a wider influence born. Moreover, in the caves at the foot of the hills,—

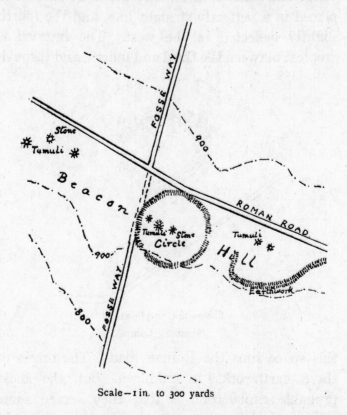

Scale—1 in. to 300 yards

at Wookey Hole, Cheddar and Banwell, have been found the earliest traces of human life in this country. Two miles from Beacon Hill stands the great earthwork of Maesbury, while continuing along the ridge, the road passes two public-houses with the unusual names of " Not Too Much " and the " Castle of Comfort." In the fields at the back of the latter inn are four remarkable circular banks and ditches, all exactly the same size, three placed in a perfectly straight line, and the fourth slightly deflected to the west. The interval is greatest between the third and fourth, and through

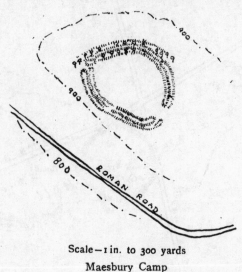

Scale—1 in. to 300 yards
Maesbury Camp

this space runs the Roman road. The origin of these earthworks is unknown, but the most probable explanation is that they served some astronomical purpose.

Weston Bay   It will be more convenient to explore the further end of the Mendips from Weston Bay, as the significance of the camps are more fully realized when approached from the sea, than from the termination of a long journey over half England.

At high water, Weston Bay is more securely enclosed than appears on the maps, as Brean Down shelters it on the south, and reaches to within three miles of Worle Hill on the north. Beyond the opening of the Bay rise the tall cliffs of the Island of Steep Holme, further off lies the

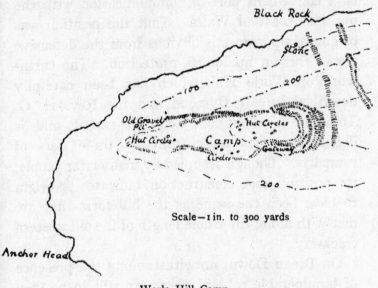

Scale—1 in. to 300 yards

Worle Hill Camp

Flat Holme, from whence it is hardly three miles to the Welsh headland, and the safe harbours of Cardiff and Barry. The whole distance is less than ten miles, and in fine weather offers a tempting passage even to the most timid. The broad sands of Weston Bay give comfortable landing to light craft, and are well protected from the N.E. and S.W. winds, whilst safety can be found within the mouth of the Axe during stress of weather from the west. The road from Winchester and Sarum to Jack Straw's Castle and the Mendips, has brought us to its termination on these shores, and their natural advantages for small ships point to the mouth of the Axe, and the sands of Weston, as a convenient port of communication with the opposite coast of Wales. That the position was of great importance is obvious from the defensive works thrown up for its protection. The earthwork on Worle Hill, which has been carefully described by Mr Dymond and the Rev. H. G. Tomkins, is about ten acres in extent, and is defended on its weak front by three tiers of ramparts. Though occupied by many later people, its position and construction indicate its origin to have been the same as the hill forts that are met with along the whole length of the old western trackway.

On Brean Down, notwithstanding the presence of innumerable rabbits, there are still to be seen the remains of a few tumuli and transverse banks and ditches. The slopes of the central and highest part, looked at from a distance, appear to have been artificially steepened, but the rocky nature of the soil and great scarcity of water, may account for the absence of any large camp.

The terminations of the Mendips as they near the sea are the site of quite a cluster of camps, as on Bleadon Hill facing south are the remains of a

Roman earthwork, and close by there are many rectangular banks that mark the position of a once extensive settlement. The summits of many of the small hills on the northern slopes are defended by circular contour forts, this northern

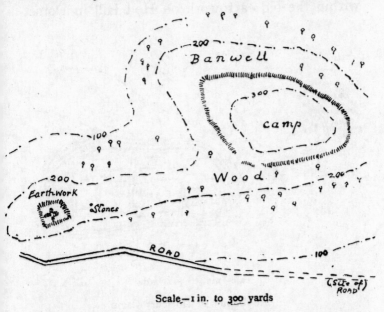

Scale—1 in. to 300 yards

line being presumably taken to avoid crossing the streams that issue from the Mendips to the south.

On the hill overlooking Banwell is situated an **Banwell Camp** oval camp of about twenty acres, enclosed by a single bank and ditch, and on the spur of the same hill is a small square earthwork, the floor of which is divided by two banks in the form of a cross.

At Rowberrow the banks are specially well pre- **Rowberrow Camp** served, and, as is quite unusual, are carried across the highest point of the hill without enclosing it. Four parallel banks divide the interior, and near the entrance is a small enclosure that has been attributed to the Romans, a far-fetched resemblance being seen between it and the Roman camp within the old earthwork on Hod Hill in Dorset-

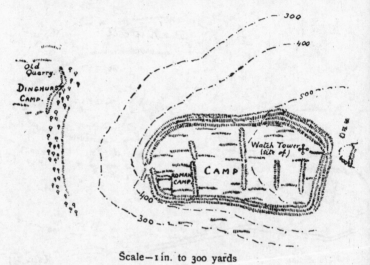

Scale—1 in. to 300 yards

Rowberrow or Dolebury Camp

shire.   Rowberrow overlooks a little valley running into the Mendips, and with a smaller camp on the opposite hill, must have afforded ample defence for the passage between them.

Burrington Camp also guards a small coombe, and the selection of these positions suggest that the camps were intended to prevent approach to the lead mines on the hills above, as well as to form convenient places for collecting merchandise.

To the north and south of the Mendips are wide stretches of low level lands, that in early times must have formed great sheets of water, since even as late as the last century, water rose at high tides as far inland as Glastonbury, and only a few years ago a Viking's boat was found in the fields near Cheddar. On the north this expanse was guarded by a camp on Cadbury Hill above Yatton, while to the south Brent Knole is crowned with fortifications.

Though perhaps the most important, Weston Bay was not the only harbour on the Severn Sea. Traces of ancient roads can be followed along the Polden Hills and the Quantocks, to meet the sea both at the mouth of the Parrett and at Watchet. In addition, north of the Bristol Avon, a line of camps from Thornbury to Almondsbury overlook the Severn, and south of the Avon, near Clevedon, stands one of the many great camps known by the name of Cadbury.

CHAPTER III

THE WATERSHED OF THE STOUR

"Where the great Vision of the guarded Mount
Looks towards Namancos and Bayona's Hold."

Camelot

FROM Jack Straw's Castle a division of the Ridgeway branches west, and following the ancient road known as the Hardway, leads ten miles away to the great camp of Camelot, or Cadbury, on the watershed of the Stour and the Parrett. Camelot, as local patriotism loves to name it, was one of the greatest fortresses in the country. Strongly placed on the summit of a steep hill, it contains about twenty acres enclosed by rows of ramparts four deep, and ditches of great depth. The position is further defended by smaller earthworks on the neighbouring hills, and by the little river Cam rising on Camel Hill which, like most of the Somersetshire rivers, was once of much greater size and importance. The slopes of the hill are covered by a wood of 'elders, and in Spring-time their scent, more subtle than hawthorn, envelops the camp with fragrance. All around is a sweeping view of Somersetshire and the Severn, with Glastonbury, where Arthur lies buried, only twelve miles away. Though Tennyson's " Many

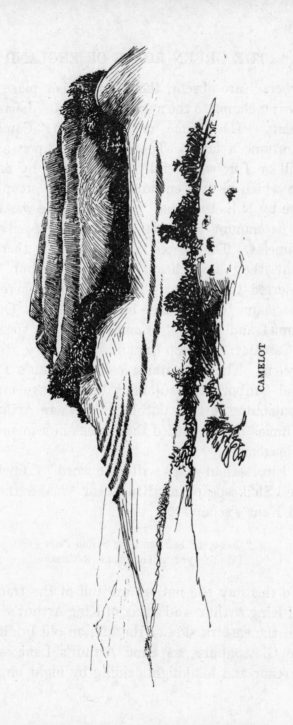

CAMELOT

towers " are absent, there is no other place with greater claims to the name of Camelot.   Leland, in Henry VIII.'s time, mentions it as " Camelette sumtyme a famose Town or Castle upon a very Hill or Tor, wonderfully strengthened by nature. To which be two entrances up a very steep way, one by N.E. the other by S.W.   There was found in Hominum Memoria a horseshoe of silver at Camelat. The people can tell nothing there but that they have heard say that Arthur much resorted to Camelat.   Divers villages there bear the name of Camalat by addition, as Queen's Camel and others."   Camden in 1586 speaks of " Camalat, a steep mountain of very difficult ascent. The inhabitants call it Arthur's Palace, and Cadbury the adjoining little village may by conjecture be that Cathbregion where Arthur (as Ninnias has it) routed the Saxons in a memorable engagement."

Elizabethan maps write the word " Camellick," and Shakespeare in " King Lear " makes the Earl of Kent exclaim—

> " Goose, if I had you upon Sarum Plain
> I'd drive you cackling home to Camelot."

To this day the natives are full of the traditions of King Arthur, and speak of King Arthur's Spring on the eastern side of the hill, an old bridle path to Glastonbury, as King Arthur's Lane, and of Arthur and his knights riding by night on horses shod with silver shoes. Arthur's Order of Knighthood was created in 497 A.D., the stations of the Round Table being Winchester, Camelot, and Caerleon. Winchester must have been given up after the fall of Old Sarum in 552, when Camelot may well have become the last stronghold of the Britons, for it was not taken till a hundred years after, and then by an army advancing from the south. Arthur, as Dr Dickenson says in " King Arthur in Cornwall," has given his name to more places in this Island than anyone except the Devil, and nowhere, not even at Tintagel, is the name of the mystic King more popular or tradition better established than at Camelot and Glastonbury. Dr Dickenson believes that the weight of evidence points to the river Camel as being the scene of Arthur's death, and gives the preference to the Cornish Camel without considering the claims of Somersetshire, though he points out the significant fact that Arthur died in 542, more than a hundred years before the Saxons are known to have penetrated into Cornwall. An alternative site is Camlan in Scotland, but as it is stated that Arthur was taken to Glastonbury after the fight and buried there, it was a long way to carry a dead or dying man. That Arthur was buried at Glastonbury is the best proof of his having lived, for in Norman days tradition of his burial was still alive, and by order of Henry II. search was made for the grave. Giraldus Cambrensis gives an account, as an eye-witness, of the finding of the body beneath a leaden cross, engraved with the following inscription,—

HIC JACET SEPULTUS INCLYTUS REX ARTHURIUS IN INSULA AVALLONIA, CUM WENNEVEREIA UXORE SUA SECUNDA

Two feet below the cross was a coffin of hollowed oak, containing the remains of a man of great stature and of a woman with golden hair. The bodies were removed to the church, and later in 1272 A.D. were again exhumed and reburied in front of the High Altar by order of Edward I. and Queen Eleanor.

Dr Dickenson says it is unusual for coffins to give their address, and that the whole story is so complete as to be suspicious. But after all Giraldus was not only no liar, but a gentleman rather opposed to the reigning family. The story also is twice confirmed, and if untrue we still have to account for the tradition that led to the search.

The camp of Camelot on its isolated height was the centre of further defences on the surrounding hills, or not impossibly these further defences were the hostile camps of attacking foes. It is all conjecture, and conjecture is all that can guide us in solving the purpose of these survivals of an extinct and unlettered past. On the south the nearest point of Corton Hill is evidently a beacon

site, still scored with ditches and terraces. The
neighbouring hill to the west is approached from
below by a deep tr ll leading to large n
the downs above, with banks now mu... .d.
In the centre of the camp are two round barrows,
with the space between almost silted up to a

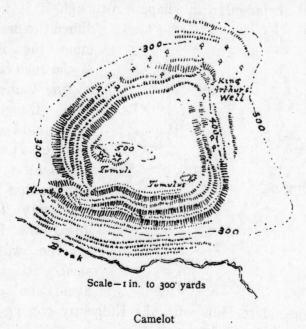

Scale—1 in. to 300 yards

Camelot

common level, and a third tumulus is prominent
at the point of the hill.

Through the enclosed and cultivated country
south of Cadbury, no trace of the ancient ridge
road can be found, but the curving watershed of
the Parrett and the Stour leads to the foot of
High Stoy and Melbury Bubb, passing camps at

Milbourne Port, Leigh Castle, and Gubbins Banks.

The shortest cut from the watershed to the Dorsetshire Hills climbs Ridge Hill past Dungeon Castle, a camp still in good preservation, and possibly of later date than the older contour forts, for it is placed on the slope of the hill, and is long, narrow and rectangular in shape. Although it is now difficult to determine the line of the road connecting Camelot with Dungeon Castle and Leigh Castle, it is reasonable to suppose that the trackway followed the line of the watershed, to join again on the

Scale—1 in to 300 yards

Leigh Castle

Dorsetshire Hills with the Ridgeway coming by way of Hanford.

It is surprising to realize that the Ridgeway from Jack Straw's Castle and Cadbury, provides communication from the Wash to the English Channel, without crossing a single river other than the Thames at Streatley, and also that it is guarded for the whole 150 miles of its course by a series of earthworks at every ten or twelve miles interval.

The modern road from Warminster to Shaftesbury runs directly south through high ground thickly scattered with tumuli. Even in early days it was hardly likely that so convenient a short cut would have been neglected, as it avoids the long detour that follows the edge of the chalk hills to Whitesheet Castle. There the roads join, and circling round the Lodden branch of the Stour, enter Shaftesbury by way of Castle Rings on Tittle Path Hill. Castle Rings is an enclosure overlooking the Semley Valley. It contains fifteen acres surrounded by a single bank and ditch, especially strong on its western side, and

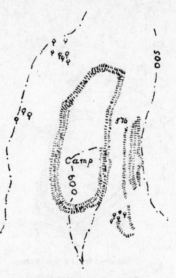

Scale—1 in. to 300 yards

Dungeon Castle

may have been a secondary camp to a neighbouring and more important fortress at Shaftesbury. Although no part of such an earthwork can now be traced, the town occupies a site identical in situation with many great contour forts. The fact that its name ends in "bury" suggests such a purpose, and on the western slopes of the promontory are undulations that appear to be remains of great ramparts.

Cranborne Chase

To the east of Shaftesbury the land between the Avon and the Stour, as far south as Badbury, was once included in Cranborne Chase, an area covering it is said 700,000 acres, and carrying

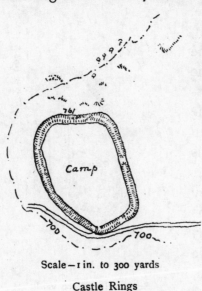

Scale — 1 in. to 300 yards

Castle Rings

twelve thousand head of fallow deer as late as 1830. With the New Forest to the southeast, and Salisbury Plain to the north, it formed an immense track of unenclosed land, which may account for the large numbers of prehistoric and Roman remains that have been preserved within its borders. It may also account for three of England's earliest antiquaries residing there, John Aubrey the " discoverer " of Avebury living at Broad Chalk, Sir Richard Colt Hoare at Stourhead, and General Pitt Rivers at Rushmore.

A high ridge runs east from Shaftesbury for ten miles between the Nadder and the Ebble, to the junction of these streams with the Avon. The old coaching road to Salisbury follows the

ridge, on either side of which there are many
tumuli and ditches, and to the north the earthworks of Castle Ditches and Chiselbury overlook
the Nadder. The old name of Castle Ditches was
Spilsbury, and it must once have been of great
strength, defended by three ramparts 40 feet high,
containing twenty-three acres. Chiselbury Camp,

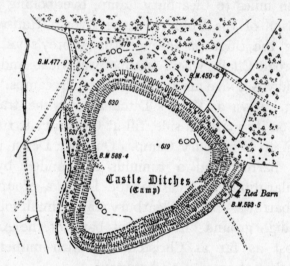

Scale—1 in. to 300 yards

a little more than three miles distant, is a single
banked enclosure of about ten acres. Two deep
trails descend to the village of Compton Chamber-
lain, indicating that busy traffic once took place
between the camp and the valley. Now little but
the tinkling of sheep-bells comes from the village
below, like the sound of running water.

South of the Ebble a second ridge road, parallel

to the first and known as the Ox Drove, passes
two tumuli at Compton Abbas, and leads to
Winklebury, a camp containing nine acres surrounded by a single ditch and bank. On the
surrounding down there are numerous entrenchments, small earthworks, and tumuli. The green
trackway runs the whole length of the ridge of
fifteen miles to Clearbury Camp, overlooking the
junction of the Ebble and the Avon. Half-way
along the ridge on the north is Aubrey's village
of Broad Chalk, where Latimer was vicar, and on
the downs above are two small Roman camps. A
ditch known as Grim's Ditch follows the track-
way on its southern side, till at Clearbury it turns
south to Whitsbury Camp. On Wick Down is a
long barrow and a tumulus surrounded by a
circular ditch, and on Charlton Down a group of
five barrows. From Clearbury many tumuli follow
the high ground on the right bank of the Avon
almost as far as Christchurch, with numerous
stretches of green road between.

The two camps at Clearbury and Whitsbury
occupy high points overlooking the Avon, and in
addition to forming defences for the river may
have served as places of safety on the journey
inland from Christchurch. Clearbury, though in
a commanding position, is only a small camp of
five acres with a single bank and ditch, but
Whitsbury, now sheltering a homestead, contains
fifteen acres enclosed by a bank of formidable

height. It was on the river below, at Charford,
that Cerdic in 508 defeated the British King Nathan
Leod, and slew five thousand of his army. Over
the river at Downton an old Folk Moot of the
Saxons remains in good preservation. The side of a
small hill can still be seen clearly cut into semi-

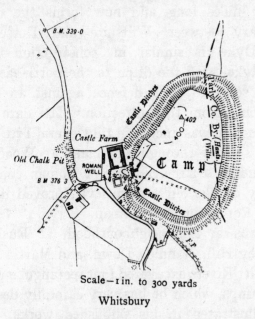

Scale—1 in. to 300 yards

Whitsbury

circular steps rising above a stretch of lawn, with
the Avon running close by, and giving convenient
approach by water.

On the high ground beyond the little river
Allen, is a pentagonal shaped camp known as
Soldiers Ring, but to what period this earthwork
belongs is not known, for it bears no resemblance
to the old contour forts, to the later camps of the

Bronze Age, or to those of the still later Romans.

Through the secluded and beautiful stretch of down between Clearbury and Pentridge, the Romans drove their road from Sarum to Badbury. It is crossed, between Blagdon Down and Vernditch Chase, by the great Bokerley Dyke which is four miles long, and now forms the county boundary between Wiltshire and Dorsetshire. The Dyke is similar in construction to the Wansdyke, with the ditch to the north-east, and would seem to be a defence against an enemy advancing from that direction. The date of its construction was uncertain till General Pitt Rivers cut a section through the bank at Woodyates, and finding a large number of Roman coins and pottery on the old surface level, proved it to be either Roman or Post-Roman.

It was in this neighbourhood, at Rushmore, Handley Hill, Handley Down, and Martin Down, that Pitt Rivers excavated four rectangular Bronze Age camps, which he has very carefully described and illustrated in his published works. These Bronze Age camps are not square like most Roman camps, but irregularly rectangular, measuring half to two acres in extent, and are generally situated on the slope of a hill. Not far from Sixpenny Handley, he minutely examined Warbarrow, a long barrow enclosed within a ditch, and after his excavations left the earth in the form of a small amphitheatre. A primary interment of the Stone Age was found in the centre of the barrow. This mound appears to have been subsequently used as an execution ground in the Romano-British period, for nineteen skeletons were found superficially buried, some with their heads off, and some with their feet.

At Bokerley Dyke the Roman road makes a slight bend in its course to Badbury, and shortly afterwards is crossed by two well-marked parallel banks that run for three miles over the downs. At their termination on Gussage Cow Down, there are two Long Barrows, and close by the site of a British village is disclosed by lines of banks and ditches a mile in length. Colt Hoare believed the parallel banks to represent a British Cursus, similar to the one near Stonehenge, and the whole site to correspond with the Roman Station of Vindogladium. Pitt Rivers, however, prefers to place this Roman Station near the bend in the Roman road close to Woodyates. After crossing the little stream between Gussage St Michael and Gussage All Saints, the Roman road ascends the steep bank to a tumulus on Holly Down, near a small Roman camp now partly destroyed by a chalk pit. To the right on Chettle Down a little to the north of the road to Blandford, are extensive remains of two British villages, and near Farnham in Bussey Stool Wood are found the remains of two small camps. At Farnham, General Pitt Rivers built his Museum, which contains many records of his work, and with his books and models, are of extreme interest to all explorers into the mysteries of British earthworks. The Roman road now passes through Crichel Park, where a branch is given off to Poole Harbour, and then continues as a broad green road over Witchampton Common to Badbury Rings.

Pentridge, lying south of the Roman road, is a strangely isolated irregular elevation, forming a natural centre between the Stour and the Avon. On its northern heights are remains of a small camp enclosed by a steep bank and ditch, with a tumulus at the highest point of its circumference, surrounded on one side by the outer ditch, and on the inner by a small ditch that cuts it off from the rest of the camp. Such arrangements are not infrequently found in old earthworks, and are perhaps the first suggestion of the Norman Motte. The trackway from Clearbury to Badbury keeps to the high ground along the back of Pentridge, and would have passed the camp, avoiding the two little Allen rivers, one running west, the other south. The direction of the ridge beyond Cranborne, with its Norman Castle, leads to Knowlton Down, where there are indications of a bank and ditch surrounding the summit. At the foot of the Down is a circular earthwork built after the pattern of Avebury Temple, with the ditch inside the bank. A large tumulus stands close by, and there is a second on the other side of the high road, while

THE TEMPLE, KNOWLE

at a little distance between the second tumulus and the Temple, is a bank at the back of some farm buildings, which once extended to the left **Knowlton Temple** of the road. In a field to the right are three more tumuli, and a line drawn through the middle of these three barrows leads to a break in the bank of the Temple, and passing through its centre, points in the direction of sunrise at Midsummer. In the centre of the Temple the ruins of a Christian church are still standing, its walls built perhaps with the same materials that once formed the stone circles of a Sun Temple.

Shaftesbury to Badbury   South of Shaftesbury the modern road runs in an identical position to the Ridgeway in the rest of its course. Following the high ground along the edge of the chalk hills above the Stour Valley, it passes tumuli on Melbury Down, and Iwerne Hill, near the commencement of Smugglers Lane. Close to the latter the Ridgeway turns to the ford across the Stour between the fortresses on Hod and Hambledon Hills, while the Badbury branch continues along the left bank of the river, passing **Pimperne** two camps, a long barrow, and at Pimperne the extensive remains of a British Settlement. Three miles from Pimperne, the high ground is occupied by Buzbury Camp. Little is left of it now save faintly marked banks, but in Warne's time it was an important earthwork, with an old trail leading from the camp to the river at Charlton Marshall. Until quite recently annual exhibitions of single-stick and wrestling took place in the enclosure.

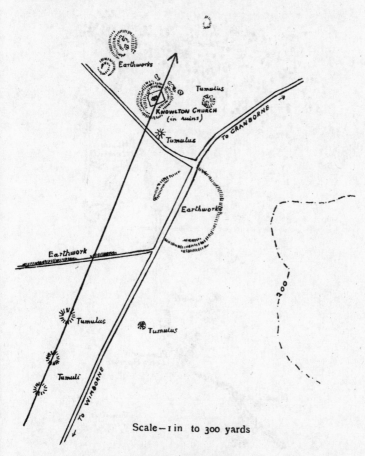

Scale—1 in to 300 yards

Knowlton Temple

From Buzbury a road runs direct to Badbury **Badbury** **Rings**, the best known and most important earthwork in this district. There is little doubt that Badbury belongs in origin to the hill forts of the

Stone Age, though occupied later by the Celtic invaders, and used by the Romans as a centre of

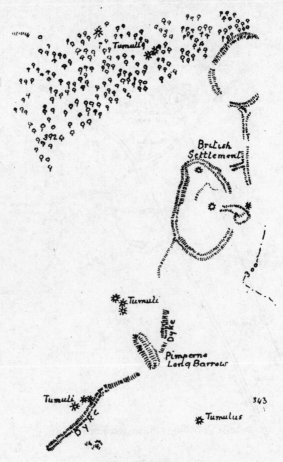

Scale—1 in. to 300 yards

Pimperne

their road system. It stands out conspicuously on the summit of a hill, defended by three tiers of banks and ditches, enclosing a space of fourteen

acres, while the middle bank with a depth of forty
feet, measures a mile in circumference. Badbury
has been claimed, though wrongly, as the scene of
Arthur's twelfth battle and fatal victory over the
Saxons in 520 A.D., and the tradition that his soul
should inhabit a raven's body " till Arthur shall
come again," has been kept alive from the fact

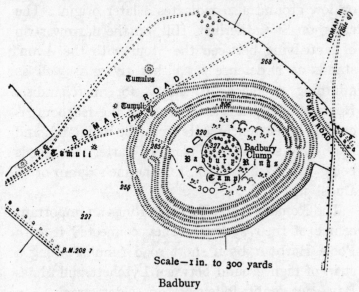

Scale—1 in. to 300 yards

Badbury

that the wood in the centre of the camp was the
last nesting place of wild ravens in England. In
Saxon times Æthelwald the Ætheling fled from
Edward the Elder, when stationed at Badbury,
to join the Danes, and it was from here also that
the clubmen of Wilts and Dorset issued their
proclamation against the Parliament.

Badbury, when first built, would have made a

convenient gathering place for traders from Christchurch or Poole Harbours.   And eight miles away
Dudsbury Camp lies by the Stour, where the banks
are steep and could have been used either as a
landing place, or a defence against the passage of
the river.   Its design is more symmetrical than is
usual with the earlier earthworks, and the position
on low ground also indicates a later origin.   The
camp on St Catherine's Hill, on the narrow strip
of land lying between the Stour with the Avon,
stands as a defence for either river, as well as
affording a place of safety for merchandise.
Hengistbury Head, to seaward of the Harbour, is
cut off by entrenchments from the mainland, and
may have served as a place of barter, the goods
being carried either to St Catherine's Camp or to
Dudsbury.

The Romans made Badbury Rings an important
centre of their system.   They connected it with
Poole Harbour by a short road running along a
strip of high ground between Lytchett and Holes
Bay, no doubt following an older track.   In
addition to the roads to Poole Harbour and Old
Sarum, a third road was carried from the camp to
Dorchester, crossing the Stour near a tumulus on
the river bank at Shapwick.

Between the Stour and Wareham the land
contains a great number of tumuli and earthworks.   Not a mile from the river crossing, Spettisbury Camp occupies the crest of a hill, and is one

of the many instances where a single banked enclosure is found not far distant from a greater fortress. Coombe Bank runs parallel to the river for some three miles over Charlton Down, and has been supposed to form a third line of defence behind the Wansdyke and Bokerley Dyke. Woolsbury Camp on Morden Heath, Woodbury Camp at Bere Regis, and Weatherby Castle, crown the highest points of land north of the harbour, and with the tumuli occupying the intervening ground, may indicate the lines taken by the old trails communicating with the sea.

Purbeck to the south of Poole Harbour, although Pu no longer an island, must at high tides before the country was drained, have been surrounded by sea, small rivers, or impassable bogs, whose waters found an exit to the Channel near Arish Mell. The island would have been a safe place to allow foreign traders to land, with Flowers Barrow—the camp above Warbarrow Bay—acting as a guard to prevent their penetrating inland, a precaution not at all unnecessary when treachery and deceit were the fine arts of savage warfare. Purbeck is almost the only place on the south coast that has not been identified with Ictis, the chief centre of the tin trade in ancient times. St Michael's Mount, the Isle of Wight, and Isle of Thanet have all been suggested by different authorities as its possible site, and though Purbeck answers the description better than most, all may well have been places of trade, for it is unreasonable to suppose that the export of tin was confined to a single port. Wareham, standing at the head of Poole Harbour, and on the point of the ridge from the Dorsetshire hills running between the Frome and the Puddle, would have

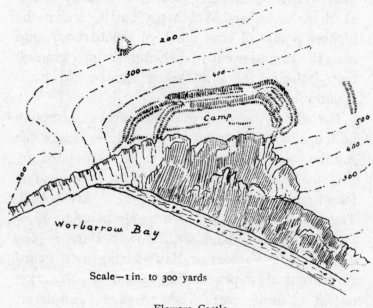

Scale—1 in. to 300 yards

Flowers Castle

formed a convenient trade depôt, with easy communication by the Ridgeway to all parts of the country. Close to the waterworks, above the town, is an odd little earthwork in the shape of a cross, from which Battery Bank and a line of tumuli, lead to Gallows Hill marked with pack-trails on the north. From this point a strip of bracken runs through the heather to the cross roads at Throop Clump. The bottom is firmer under the bracken than the heather, and as it keeps to the slightly higher ground, would appear to be the original line of traffic. From the cross roads a succession of tumuli follow the ridge as far as Puddletown, and from there the ridge road can be traced past Robin's Barrow. Beyond more tumuli, a British village, and a small earthwork, it joins the hill road from Dorchester to Sherbourne, and makes connection with the Ridgeway opposite the trail from Dungeon Castle.

The date of the walls of Wareham has never been determined, and how long ago the trade in tin began it is impossible to say. M. Reinach gives proof of its being carried on by the Phrygians about 900 B.C., and it may well go back to the commencement of the Bronze Age in this country. But before the discovery of tin, men went down to the sea in ships, and situated at the terminus of an important ridge road, on a safe and sheltered harbour, it is possible that Wareham was a seaport as far back as the Stone Age.

CHAPTER IV

THE DORSETSHIRE HILLS

" There is a thirst in my soul for the fair free spaces
of infinite distance. . . ."

EIGHT miles south from Shaftesbury the
Ridgeway turns west near two tumuli on
Iwerne Hill, and following the line of
Smugglers Lane, passes between the great fortresses
on Hod and Hambledon Hills. The only ford for
some miles, either up or down the Stour, lies
directly below these two formidable entrenchments,
which must have effectually guarded the river
crossing, and secured the main gateway into the
down country, as well as keeping strict watch
over Blackmoor Vale to the west.

Hod Hill Camp   Hod Hill towers high above the Stour, its tall
cliffs drooping sheer from the camp to the river
below. The plateau at the top of the hill measures
some fifty acres, and is enclosed by double and
sometimes triple ramparts and ditches. Within
the area are still to be traced many pit dwellings,
and some curious little circular earthworks with
openings to the south and west. A square of
seven acres, at the north-west corner, has been cut
off from the rest of the camp by two rectangular

HANFORD WITH HOD AND HAMBLEDON HILL CAMPS

ramparts with openings in their centre. These inner banks are certainly of later date than the outer defences, and are due either to Roman occupation of the old native fortress, or to the adoption by the British of the Roman construction, after their late Masters had left the country. Many flint instruments and Roman coins have from time to time been found on Hod Hill, some of which are now exhibited in the British Museum.

Hambledon Hill Camp A mile and a half distant, on Hambledon Hill, is an even larger camp, enclosed by a single rampart and ditch nearly two miles in circumference; the interior is divided by a transverse ditch, and has a conspicuous tumulus standing on the centre of the ridge. The last act of war witnessed by this formidable fortress can hardly have been of such a savage nature as its earlier fortunes, for it was here in 1645 that the Rector of Compton, with two thousand men, bid defiance to Cromwell, and necessitated the storming of the hill by Colonel Desborough. Seen from below the great length of entrenchment is most imposing, and with the similar camp on Hod Hill, must have been constructed for some strategic purpose of the first importance. It is not unlikely that the division between the chalk downs and the Dorsetshire Hills was a tribal boundary, the two great Camps guarding the entrance into the down country, and perhaps at the same time preventing the passage

of raiders up the river from Christchurch.   If the
Ridgeway, true to its course, continued to follow
the line of great earthworks, it would have passed
between these two fortresses, have crossed the river
ford, and gained the high Dorsetshire Hills.   The

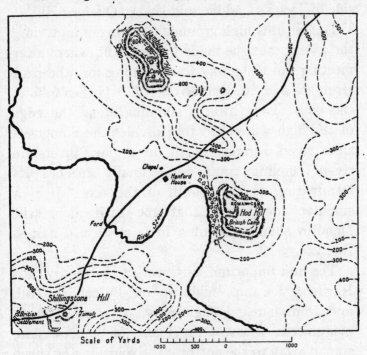

Hod Hill and Hambledon Hill

ford now lies in the grounds of Hanford (old ford)
House, the seat of the Ker Seymers, but there is
nothing to suggest in its present peaceful surroundings that it was once a busy centre on the most
important road in the Kingdom.   Five thousand
years have effectually smoothed away all traces

of traffic in the valley bottom, though it would be interesting to know what the dredging of the river at this point might disclose.   Immediately beyond the ford the ground rises by a spur of down to Shillingstone Hill, where pack-trails ascend by the side of Jacob's Ladder, and lead to Okeford Hill.

To gain this high ground, if driving or motoring, the ascent must be made by Bell Hill, where after meeting the Ridgeway from Shillingston, the road stretches away to Bulbarrow Hill.   It then follows the lines of earthworks standing along the edge of the high watershed that divides the Somerset-shire rivers running north, from the Dorsetshire rivers running south, and finally reaches its termination at the mouth of the Axe.   It is a singular coincidence that the road along the Mendips should end at a little river also named the Axe.

Rawlsbury Camp

The first important earthwork to be met with is Rawlsbury Camp, high up on Bulbarrow Hill, and from here to High Stoy, nine miles away, magnificent views of the Plains of Somersetshire spread away to the north.   The solitude, the sheep on the hillside, rabbits playing on the road, and a fox looping through the heather, hardly suggest that we are on the line of a once important high-way.   But its course can be traced past earthworks and tumuli, almost the earliest signs left us of that never-ending struggle we call evolution.   Above Melcombe Park, at Dorsetshire Gap, a short length of earthwork looks as if it might have once enclosed Nutcombe Tout, and a tumulus close at hand, marks the direction of pack-trails ascending its southern slope. On Church Hill a mile or so further, at the edge of Bloody Tent Wood, is a small square camp, probably Roman, while the hillside itself is marked with the pits and irregular banks of a British village. Barnet Lane leads from Church Hill to a tumulus on Little Minterne Hill, placed just beyond the Sherborne and Dorchester road. Near this tumulus, on Revel's Hill,

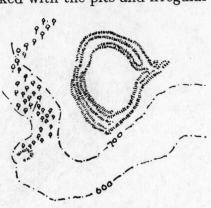

Scale — 1 in. to 300 yards

Rawlsbury Camp

the road from Camelot climbs Ridge Hill, passes Dungeon Camp, and then unites with the Ridgeway, at the point where the trail from Wareham joins it from the opposite direction. From near the junction a considerable ditch runs across the northern face of Minterne Hill to Dogberry Down, where in a wood above Lyons Gate, the remains of a circular camp can still be traced. The Ridgeway now circles round to the south of High Stoy, passing a tumulus on the way to Up Cerne Wood, where it is crossed by a trans-

verse ditch, and is then continued to a tumulus on
Batcombe Hill near the " Cross and Hand " Inn.
The Roman road from Dorchester to Ilchester
follows the ridge of Batcombe Hill, and on either
side are many tumuli and remains of a British
Settlement.   The line of the watershed is traced

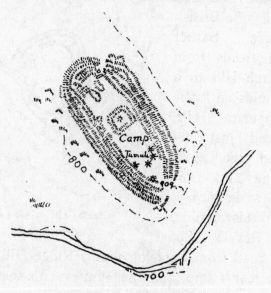

Scale — 1 in. to 300 yards

Pilsdon Pen

to Holy Well, Evershot, Toller Down Gate, and
the Hoar Stone.   From the Hoar Stone a branch
road is given off in the direction of Eggardon
Hill, and the Ridgeway, leaving the main western
Watershed, follows the high ground forming the
watershed of the Axe and the Brit, the former
rising on Beaminster Down between east and west

Noller Farms on the right, and the latter on Whitesheet Hill, to the left. Before reaching Broad Windsor the road turns south to Clan Hill,

Lambert's Castle.

Waddon Hill, Lewesdon Hill and Pilsdon Pen. Lewesdon Hill, nine hundred and sixty feet above the sea level, is the highest point in Dorsetshire, and gives magnificent views over Eggardon and the whole country to the south. At Broad Windsor, Fuller, the author of " English Worthies," was Vicar, and it was here that Charles II. took refuge after the battle of Worcester, a dangerous refuge, however, for the inhabitants were disloyal, and afterwards became hot supporters of Monmouth.

Pilsdon Pen Camp

The camp on Pilsdon Pen, placed on the highest point of the hill, is nine acres in extent, enclosed

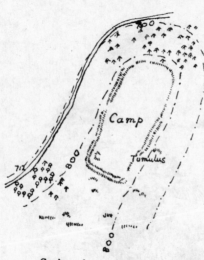

Scale—1 in. to 300 yards
Lambert's Castle

by triple banks and ditches. In the centre is a rectangular enclosure containing a tumulus, and at the southern end there are four more tumuli. On the northern slopes at Race Down House, Wordsworth and his sister lived for some time. From Pilsdon Pen the road passes the Standing Stone on Sliding Hill, and runs to the " Rose and Crown " at Birdsmoor Gate, where turning south it leaves Bettiscombe on the left, and reaches Lambert's Castle. Lambert's or Lammas Castle, encloses twelve acres with triple banks and ditches following the eight hundred foot contour.

Coney's Castle, a little to the south, stands on the six hundred foot contour, with three banks and ditches defending it on the east. On the west, however, where the hill side drops sharply, it is guarded by a single ditch. The southern portion of the camp is separated from the rest by a bank and

ditch, the whole camp measuring about nine acres. It was here that Egbert had his headquarters in 883 A.D. when defeated by the Danes at Charmouth.

From Lambert's Castle the Ridgeway takes the Axminster road along Stone Barrow Hill, turning at Hunter's Lodge to follow the ridge that ends at Charton Bay, and forms the termination of the chalk hills of England.

Scale—1 in. to 300 yards
Coney's Castle

Less than two miles directly west of Trinity Beacon, standing on the line of the Foss Way, is Aske House, where the Duke of Marlborough was born. From a tumulus on Shapwick Hill, a road known as Fire Barrow Lane, branches off to Musbury Camp, an irregular enclosure with an area of six acres. **Musbury Camp** Two miles further, above the village of Axemouth, Hawkesdown Camp stands, overlooking the harbour. Nothing to-day could look less like an important harbour than the mouth of the Axe, for its tiny stream struggles with difficulty between cliff and shingle to reach the sea. Yet as recently as William III.'s reign, ships traded here from distant countries, and though now the little bay is silted up, it is admirably sheltered from rough weather. If sea-going vessels could have unloaded here little more than two hundred years ago, it is easy to believe that prehistoric shipping would have found it a commodious harbour. Musbury and Hawkesdown were a protection on the east, forming perhaps depôts for goods whilst waiting the convenience of shipping.

Scale—1 in. to 300 yards

Musbury

Branscombe and Black-bury Castles To the west of the harbour, Branscombe Castle on the coast, Blackbury Castle to the north of the Exeter road, and Sidbury Castle, may have served a similar purpose. There are four camps, Widworthy, Broadhayes, Membury and the camp above Yarcombe, standing on the ridges leading

north to the watershed on the Blackdown Hills.
It must have been along these ridges that communication was
made with the
watershed,
leading to the
Bristol Channel
near Bude, and
further on into
Cornwall. Be-
tween Axe-
mouth and
Seaton, was the
site of the
Roman station of Muridunum, from which the
Romans carried their great Foss Way inland to

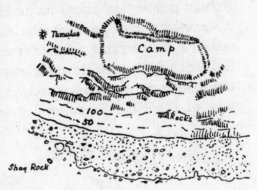

Scale—1 in. to 300 yards

Branscombe Castle

Lincoln, keeping almost
parallel with the ridge
road along the chalk
downs and the Cots-
wold Hills.

The Dorsetshire Hills,
between the Ridgeway
and the sea, form an
intricate jumble of hills
of which hardly one
is not crowned with

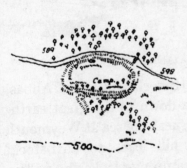

Scale—1 in. to 300 yards

Blackbury Castle

tumuli, or " Marys " as they are called hereabout,
the banks of earthworks, the terracing of ancient
cultivation, cromlechs, pit-dwellings or hut circles.

These signs that remain to us prove that the land must have been densely populated with some Pre-Roman people, and the Romans themselves found it necessary to open out the fastnesses of the country by carrying roads through the district. Eggardon Hill, with its great camp, is the key of the situation. A trail connects it with the Ridge-way at the Hoar Stone, and a second trail may

Cerne Abbas

be followed through Cattistock and Cerne Abbas, whilst a third road runs down to the great earth-work named the Maiden, near the sea at Weymouth Bay. A long spur of hill leads to Cattistock, where a small circular camp overlooks the valley. The green road then crosses the downs to Cerne Abbas, where there are two more small camps, and where on the slopes of the hill the " Wild Man " is cut in the chalk. He belongs to an uncouth generation, but the anatomy is a little too perfect to be attributed to the same artistic inspiration that carved the White Horse on Uffington Hill.

Eggardon Camp encloses twenty acres and is **Eggardon Camp** situated on the hill overlooking Powerstock, the steep slopes on three of its sides being

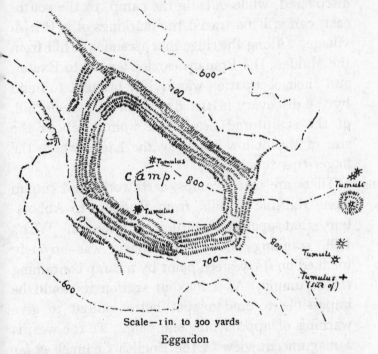

Scale—1 in. to 300 yards

Eggardon

strengthened by three strong ramparts. On the fourth side it is divided from the down by a narrow neck of land defended by only two ramparts, with a singularly broad space between them. At the edge of the spur stands a tumulus which has been very thoroughly opened and left neglected. A small secondary spur of down juts out from the camp to the north east, but is not enclosed within the ramparts. Eggardon must have been a populous centre for long periods of time, for inside the camp are many pit-dwellings, on the floors of which no sign of metal has been discovered, while outside the camp, to the south-east, can still be traced the markings of a British village. Along the ridge that ascends the hill from the Maiden, the Romans carried a road to Exeter, and their occupation was vividly brought to mind by the discovery in the dry earth of a mole hill, of the sculptured head of a woman, about the size of the hollow made by the hands where the finger-tips touch.

Wears Hill Camp
There are many camps, earthworks and tumuli along the line of hills, from Bridport to Abbotsbury, that separate Eggardon from the sea. Wears Hill, standing above Abbotsbury, was strongly fortified on its western point by a camp containing three tumuli. As a lookout station it would be impossible to find a spot better suited to give warning of approaching shipping. To the west is a magnificent view of the English Channel as far as the coast of Devon, and immediately below, the Chesil Beach with its strip of enclosed water, stands out so clearly that on fine days not a coracle could move without being seen. At the head of the water are two small hills surrounded with the terracings, and on the summit of one stands the ruined chapel of St Catherine. To the south-

east is a splendid view of Weymouth Bay, and immediately in front stretches away the great headland of Portland.

Weymouth Bay, the waters of the Fleet, and Portland, form just such a combination as was adapted for savage trading. The shelving sands of the bay are the finest in the west country, and make easy landing from open boats. In rough

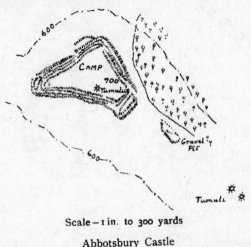

Scale — 1 in. to 300 yards

Abbotsbury Castle

weather The Fleet offers perfect shelter, and, on Portland, trading could take place without allowing strangers dangerous access to the mainland.

Between Wears Hill and the Hardy Monument on Black Down, are the remains of a Stone Circle, some pit dwellings, two cromlechs known as " The Grey Mare and her Colts" and the " Hell Stone." From Black Down a green road follows a long line of hills overlooking Weymouth Bay, and passing

through Waddon, Upwey, and Poxwell, leads
direct to the Isle of Purbeck, at the point below
Flowers Barrow Camp, which crests the cliffs of
Warbarrow Bay. About mid-distance Chalbury

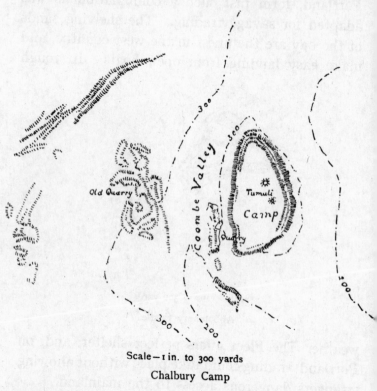

Scale—1 in. to 300 yards

Chalbury Camp

Camp crowns a small hill just north of Preston,
approached by a valley with lynchetts on either
side, and named by a former generation of soldiers
" Balaclava," from its resemblance to that famous
and fatal valley. The camp itself is enclosed in a
single bank and ditch, and contains many good

specimens of pit dwellings. The whole range of
hills is studded by numerous large tumuli arranged
singly or in groups, and for the most part standing
out clearly on the sky-line. A collection of six

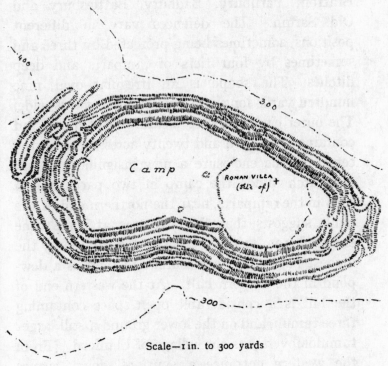

Scale—1 in. to 300 yards

The Maiden

are specially prominent on the ridge above Brin-
combe, three with flattened and three with rounded
tops.

Behind this long ridge, on a low hill
two miles from _Dorchester, stands Maiden
Castle, the most astounding earthwork in the

country. Its great banks and ditches, and the
extreme complexity of its entrances, leave us
marvelling at the ingenuity and labour of its construction, even after familiarity with Avebury,
Bratton, Yarnbury, Badbury, Battlesbury and
Old Sarum. The defences vary in different
positions, sometimes being protected by three and
sometimes by four tiers of ramparts and deep
ditches. The shape is an irregular oval, nine
hundred yards long and four hundred yards wide.
The outer circumference measures two miles, and
contains a hundred and twenty acres. Across the
centre of the enclosure a now insignificant bank
and ditch divide the camp in two parts, and a
turn in the ramparts, near the northern end of the
bank, suggests that the area was at some time
enlarged from this point. Two tumuli occupy the
highest part of the enclosure, and there is a dew-
pond in the western half. At the western end of
the hill is a considerable open space containing
three tumuli, and on the lower ground a still larger
tumulus overlooks the village of Clanford. From
the western entrance a spur of down curves
between the earthwork and the sea, the track-
way along its brow being marked with tumuli.
If Weymouth Bay, as we have supposed, was
used as a trading centre, it was along this little
ridge of down that communication between the
sea and the Maiden was most easy. Within the
great fortress the treasures of commerce could

THE MAIDEN. SOUTHERN RAMPARTS

be held secure, while so great a warehouse destroys any idea that it was necessary for merely trifling trade. The situation, commanded by higher ground both on the north and south, cannot have been selected wholly for defence. Its very size must have been a weakness if seriously assaulted, since it would have required an army for its protection. A few guards patrolling the ramparts, would, however, give security against marauders to traders and caravans whilst waiting within the camp, though such dangers must have been heavy enough to require these immense banks and ditches to secure their safety.

Below the northern rampart are two tumuli, and an earthwork that appears to have been connected with the camp. It is here also that commences the long straight ascent of ten miles, that connects the Maiden with Eggardon. The modern road follows pretty much the Roman, as the Roman no doubt followed an earlier trackway, and reaches the crest of the hill near a dewpond between two tumuli a little south of the camp. From Eggardon, as we have seen, there is a choice of routes to the Ridgeway, where a trader would have access to the whole interior of the country.

The construction of so huge an earthwork as the Maiden is sufficient proof that unsual importance was attached to the district, and whatever may have been the reason, it did not cease when its builders departed. The Celts who succeeded them also built their great camp close by at Poundbury, and these departing in their turn, the Romans founded a settlement in the same neighbourhood at Dorchester.

Poundbury is a rectangular camp overlooking Poundbury the Frome, having no bank or ditch on the river Camp side, which is sufficiently defended by the steep cliff. Here, however, a ledge has been formed to give secure footing to the defenders, and this footway continues along the bank far up the valley, always keeping about the same level above the river. On the remaining three sides of the camp there are indications of double banks and ditches, but on only one are they in good preservation, though the main rampart stands out boldly and distinctly on all three of them, and a large tumulus occupies the highest point in the camp. The hill beyond is cut by a transverse ditch, and the ascent from the west is marked by pack-trails running parallel to the modern road.

On both sides of the Frome are many remains of earthworks. There are signs of a second camp near Poundbury, another above Charminster, and to the east of Dorchester on Mount Pleasant are the remains of a circular bank, whilst Maumbury Ring, lying between the G.W. and S.W. Railways, has, after recent investigations, been pronounced to be a Roman Amphitheatre built on the site of an early temple.

CHAPTER V

SALISBURY PLAIN AND STONEHENGE

" To-morrow to fresh woods and pastures new."

BETWEEN the Avon and the Wylye lies the heart of Salisbury Plain, and two miles from Amesbury in the fork of the roads to Warminster and Devizes, stands Stonehenge, its greatest treasure. Dwarfed in the wide expanse of open country, the first sight of Stonehenge is disappointing, for neither the stones nor the circle are as impressive as the image left on the imagination by old pictures and the thought of its mystery. Wonder grows with familiarity. For centuries many minds have given themselves to the effort of reconstructing the plan on which these stones were arranged, and in explaining their purpose. It was only after the gradual unfolding of the existence of a Stone Age, and the light thrown by recent investigations on Greek and Egyptian Sun Temples, that success could reward the inquiry.

The researches of Sir Norman Lockyer, Mr Penrose and Professor Gowland come from such high authority, that the results they have obtained may be taken as all that can at present be unravelled, making it unnecessary seriously to consider the earlier theories put forward. The first written mention, believed to refer to Stonehenge, was made in the year 400 B.C. by Hecateus, a Greek, who states that " The Hyperboreans have in their Island a sacred enclosure dedicated to Apollo, as well as a magnificent circular temple adorned with rich offerings." In modern times Dr John Smith, 1771, was the earliest writer with sufficient insight to point out that Stonehenge was a temple used for explaining the heavenly bodies.

The havoc of centuries has reduced Stonehenge to little more than a ruin. Only seventeen great stones out of forty retain their position, and the work of destruction continued till the stormy last night of the last century, when another of the great stones fell to the ground. Since the tall " Leaning Stone," as it was then called, was threatened with a similar fate, the Society of Antiquaries, and the Wiltshire Archæological Society, replaced it during the following year in its upright position, the work being carried out under the supervision of Professor Gowland. During the operations it was discovered that the method of erecting the great stones was to slide them down the inclined side of a hole in the chalk, then raise them against the opposite vertical side, and for greater security to pack the base with flints, broken blue-stones, worn-out flint axes and hammer stones. The use of these instruments indicated that the Stone Age lasted as late as the erection of the temple.

The stone temple is enclosed within a circular bank and ditch 300 feet in diameter, the circle being broken for fifty feet, where the banks turn to form the sides of the avenue and are continued across the downs towards the north east. In this opening of the circle lies the flat " Slaughter Stone," and a little way down the Avenue stands the rough upright Pointer Stone, known as the Friar's Heel. Within the circle are two tumuli close to the bank, one a little east of south, the other just west of north ; to the N.W. and S.E. are two rough stones also close to the bank. These banks are much less distinct now than even in Sir Richard Colt Hoare's time, a hundred years ago, and are likely with the increasing traffic of the Plain to become fainter every year.

In the centre of the circular bank stood the Temple, its outer wall being built of thirty tall Sarsen Stones placed four feet apart, and connected above by massive horizontal stone lintels, giving the structure the solid appearance of Egyptian architecture. Within this stone circle were five trilithons of even larger stones, gradually increasing in height towards the east, and arranged in the shape of a horse shoe, the open end facing the Avenue, with the immense recumbent altar stone lying in front of the centre trilithon. Unlike the great Sarsens at Avebury these upright stones are tooled to an even surface and carefully squared, with projections left for securing the lintels. Between the circle of great stones and the five trilithons, and again between the horse shoe and

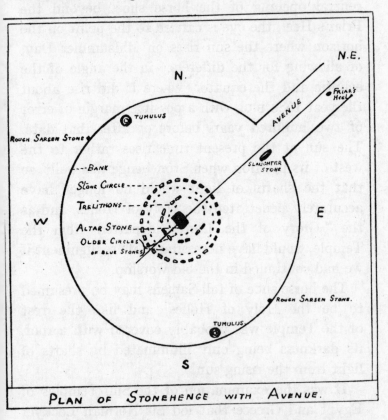

PLAN OF STONEHENGE WITH AVENUE.

the altar stone, are the remains of two smaller circles of upright blue stones, entirely different in character to the large Sarsen stones. Sir Norman Lockyer considers them to be connected with a worship older than that associated with the larger circle and to have relation with the rough unhewn Friar's Heel, and the two recumbent Sarsen stones at the north-west and south-east of the circular bank. Looking down the Avenue through the central opening of the horse shoe, beyond the Friar's Heel, the eye is carried to the point on the horizon where the sun rises on Midsummer Day, or allowing for the difference in the angle of the ecliptic and the equator, where it did rise about the year 1680 B.C., with a possible margin of error of two hundred years before or after that date. The sun at the present time rises rather to the west of its position when Stonehenge was built, so that the shafts of light would no longer have accurately penetrated the Holy of Holies, and as the " Glory of the Lord " departed from the Temple, would have necessitated its realignment if we had continued in the old worship.

The horse shoe of tall Sarsens may be presumed to be the Holy of Holies, and like the rest of the Temple was probably covered with a roof, its darkness being only illuminated by shafts of light from the rising sun.

It was the examination of the Sun Temples of Egypt and Greece that led Sir Norman Lockyer and Mr Penrose to investigate the age of Stonehenge, and its probable use as a Sun Temple. Sir Norman Lockyer says that the earliest known orientation of Egyptian temples for agricultural purposes dates from 6400 B.C. and pointed to the star Canopus, corresponding to the fall of the Nile, or the commencement of seed-time. Subsequently the orientation of the Temples and Pyramids was varied to other stars, or to the sun at different times of the year. Although in this country there were no such magnificent temples as Karnac, Thebes, or Memphis, there are many humble stone circles in Britain fulfilling a similar purpose, as at Stanton Drew, and Rollright, the Stienes in Orkney, and the Hurlers in Cornwall. Indeed so numerous are they that almost every little community seems to have possessed its local Temple. The orientation varied according to the gods to be propitiated, the older examples corresponding to the Flower Year from May to November, Stonehenge being altered to the Solstitial year from June to December, whilst others observed the Equinoctial year, from March to September, or the Harvest year from August to February. Sir Norman Lockyer believes there is evidence to suggest that the circles of small blue stones were first arranged to indicate the May to November year, and to be of considerably earlier date than the circle of great Sarsens, and that Stonehenge was built at different times is probable from the stone circles and the earth circle all having different centres. The dates for commencing the various years would be ascertained by watching the rise of different stars, and it may be that some of the numerous tumuli occupying the ridges of down close to Stonehenge, and standing out sharply against the sky-line, served as sight lines for this purpose. It is not necessary to take the details of these conclusions too literally, for indeed they have been subjected to rather damaging criticism, and the inhabitants of Stonehenge four thousand years ago were probably content with much rougher calculations than modern mathematicians. The Friar's Heel may or may not be in its right place, or it may be only one of two stones, with a slit between them for observing the sun, and the blue stones may or may not have been erected before the great circle. These details must be more or less guesswork, but there the Stone Circle stands, with its avenue pointing to the rising sun, and even the most critical do not pretend that its plan is the result of accident.

What connection, if any, the Druids had with Stonehenge, is very obscure, for it is necessary to remember that the country was occupied by two successive Celtic invasions between the building of Stonehenge and the period when we have written records of Druid practices. In Cæsar's time the religious ceremonies of Germany appear more in accord with the older worship in this country than the Druidical practices he observed in Britain.

M. Reinach says that, from all we know of Druidism, it appears to have been polydemonous, chiefly concerned with elves, gnomes, dwarfs, fairies and bogies. In this country hares, geese and the cock were held sacred, the tradition that the cock served as a protection against thunderstorms, possibly accounting for its image still being used on our church steeples, while, in the depths of the country, hare's brains are even to this day believed to be of great benefit to ailing new-born babes. The Celtic festival of Midsummer Day, when peasants made their animals jump through bonfires may have been connected with sun worship, and possibly it was the survival of some such festival that gave the opportunity for the murder, one May day at Stonehenge, of 460 British chiefs by the Saxons, which seems to have been an inglorious incident of their conquest.

The Druids themselves were a national clergy, recruited from the noble youths of the country, possessing great power and influence. But the priesthood does not appear to have held absolute power, for at Cæsar's coming it was the tribal chiefs who were in command, and who fought against him, the government being no longer a pure theocracy as it probably was in the early days when Avebury was a great Sun Temple.

The Avenue from Stonehenge stretches in a north-easterly direction for 600 yards, where Stukeley says in his time it divided into two branches, one ascending the hill on the right to the long line of tumuli on the ridge above Vespasian's Camp, the other passing through the

The Cursus Cursus in the valley, but all traces of these branches are now destroyed. It is doubtful to what period the Cursus belongs, though it is generally believed to be Roman, and may certainly be considered the oldest racecourse in the country. It is a perfectly straight enclosure, a mile and five furlongs in length, and a hundred yards wide. The western end, containing two tumuli, is cut off from the remainder of the course by a transverse bank, and may have been used for giving the final preparations to the horses and chariots. Outside the east end is a raised bank, affording a good view of the finish, and, as the Cursus lay in the Valley, an unlimited number of spectators could view the racing from the hill sides.

Tumuli There still remain an immense number of tumuli of all ages scattered over Salisbury Plain ; long chambered barrows of the Neolithic times, round barrows marking the trackways, barrows of the Bronze Age used for simple earth burials, and after the introduction of cremation barrows, for burials in cinerary urns, post Roman barrows, and barrows with Saxon burials. These are chiefly arranged in groups, all varieties being mingled together, and occupying for the most part the sky-line of the different ridges. The largest collection is found in the immediate neighbourhood of Stonehenge, where it would be interesting to investigate the possibility of their being used as sight lines for observing the stars. The long barrows are specially numerous round Tilshead, at the head of the Shrewton valley, where the spurs of down are concentrated as to the centre of a circle, and appear to have been the site of very early occupation.

Ell Barrow and Knighton Barrow are both conspicuous long barrows and useful landmarks, for there is hardly any part of the Plain from which one or the other cannot be seen by mounting the nearest ridge. To the earliest inhabitants they must have been of assistance in finding the trackways across the downs, and are a help even now to anyone fairly acquainted with the lie of the land.

In the early part of the nineteenth century Sir Richard Colt Hoare and Mr Cunnington opened some two hundred of these tumuli, and were the first to make a serious study of British Barrows. Their "finds" consisted chiefly of flint arrow heads, and polished celts, bronze ornaments and weapons, glass and amber beads, bone pins, cinerary urns, burnt human bones, bones of animals, stags' horns, and now and then gold ornaments, drinking cups, and incense bowls, many of which are beautifully illustrated in Hoare's " Ancient Wiltshire," and may be seen in the British Museum and the museums at Devizes and Salisbury.

How dense the population must once have been Population upon the Plain is shown by its numerous earthworks, and the remains of villages that can still be traced upon the down surface. These villages are no longer simple collections of pit-dwellings, but are marked by numerous rectangular banks, where the turf is finer and greener than on the open down, and in their neighbourhood long ditches and small earthworks are frequent.   Vestiges of such villages are found at Durrington Walls on the Avon, on Winterbourne Stoke Down, on Breakheart Hill, on Chitter Down, and to the north of Imber. The banks of the small earthworks are often very indistinct, and vary greatly in shape.   They are found on the ridge south of Stonehenge, the hills round Tilshead, at Rollestone, and to the east of the Devizes road, where a curious small double circle can still be seen on Alton Down.   North of Chittern St Mary is an earthwork known as Knock Castle, and near it are the remains of two British villages connected by a ditch known as the " old ditch."   Close by have been found many Roman coins of Vespasian, Antonius and Trajan, together with iron nails, hinges, keys and rough Roman pottery.

Vespasian's Camp   The road from Stonehenge to Amesbury cuts through the high ramparts of an earthwork known as Vespasian's Camp.   The name can have little to do with its origin, for the earthwork resembles a British hill-fort much more closely than a Roman camp, though it is quite possible that Vespasian occupied it.   The earthwork is long and narrow, enclosing some thirty-nine acres, and stands almost due north and south, with either

end overlooking the Avon, completely cutting
off the long stretch of meadow-land enclosed by
the loop of the river. Towards Stonehenge it is
strongly defended by a high bank and ditch, and
is admirably placed, not only for its own protec-

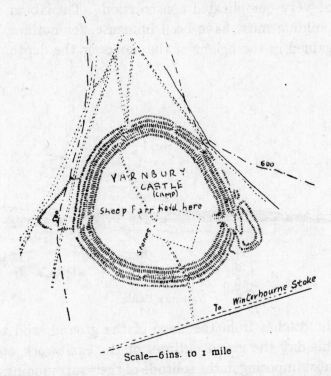

Scale—6 ins. to 1 mile

tion, but for securing its food supply by giving
safety to the cattle in the meadows enclosed by
the river.

. Six miles west of Stonehenge, just north of the
road to Wylye and Warminster, the still more
imposing earthwork of Yarnbury stands out boldly

from a level plateau of high down. Triple banks
and ditches enclose an area of twenty-eight acres,
while the outer ditch is a mile in length, the
height of the vallum fifty feet, and the entrance
to the east defended by a detached earthwork
of very complicated construction. The labour of
building must have been immense, for nothing is
gained in the height of the banks or the depth of

Yarnbury Castle

the ditches from the slope of the ground, and to
this day the grand outlines of the earthwork are
most imposing in the solitude of their surroundings.

Codford Ring Codford Ring is situated nearly four miles west
of Yarnbury, at the junction of a small stream
from Chittern with the Wylye. It resembles those
single-banked enclosures frequently found in the
neighbourhood of great fortresses, and which it
has been suggested, may have been used as their

cattle compounds. The circle encloses an area of nine acres, has easy access to water, and can be clearly seen from Yarnbury.

To the extreme north of the plain, overlooking the Pewsey Valley, are Casterley Castle and Broadbury Banks, two earthworks on the line of the great trackway running east to Inkpen Beacon. Casterley Castle is a large enclosure of

Casterley and Broadbury

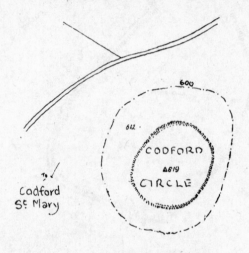

Scale—6 ins. to 1 mile

over sixty acres, defended by a single bank and ditch. It is large enough to have formed an enclosed village and may have served as a halting-place for travellers crossing the Avon, just as Chisenbury Camp, on the opposite side of the river, may have offered similar shelter. Broadbury Banks are situated on the edge of the hills on the line of the southern branch of the Ridgeway as it rises from the Pewsey Valley, and though its banks are now rather dilapidated, the pack-trails on the hills side show that it was once the site of important traffic.

Trackways   A branch of the Ridgeway can be traced from

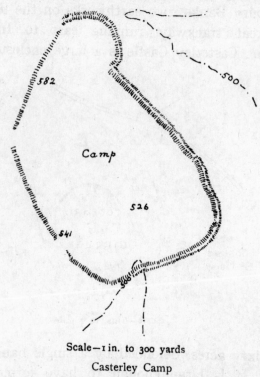

582

Camp

526

541

Scale—1 in. to 300 yards

Casterley Camp

Broadbury to Ell Barrow, and then along the ridge, east of the Devizes road, to Knighton Barrow and Stonehenge. A little further it divides into two branches, one going to Old Sarum and the other to Stapleford. On the right bank of the stream at Stapleford is a small earthwork, giving protection to a ford that must have been of considerable importance, as a second trackway coming from Yarnbury also crosses at this point, making probably for Old Sarum. North of Yarnbury this trail is continued as a green road to Warminster and Bratton, and is known as the Bath Drove Road. Beside these two trackways running north and south, there are many trails crossing the Plain from east to west, as from Tilshead to Knighton, and Tilshead to Enford, from Shrewton to Bulford, and Yarnbury to Shrewton.

CHAPTER VI

OLD SARUM

" There was a day when they were young and proud.
    Banners on high, and battles passed below;
But they who fought are in a bloody shroud,
    And those who waved are shredless dust ere now."

NEAR Salisbury four tributaries join the river Avon—the Bourne from the east, and the Wylye, the Nadder, and the Ebble from the west. They then continue their united course until the Avon meets the Stour at Christchurch. Twelve miles east of Salisbury the Test runs south to empty itself into Southampton Water, and further east again, the Itchen runs a parallel course through Winchester to Southampton. Scattered among the downs that give rise to these little rivers are innumerable remains of a civilization that existed at a period of which tradition has no suspicion, and history no record. It was not until the middle of the nineteenth century that serious study was given to the earthworks and flint instruments, that gradually revealed the secrets of the Stone Age. These evidences are found in greater abundance among these now thinly populated chalk hills, than in any other part of England.

OLD SARUM

Old Sarum   Old Sarum, two miles north of Salisbury, and four from Stonehenge, appears to have been the centre of the district. It has a longer and more continuous story than any other place in English History, playing an important part from pre-historic times to the nineteenth century. The earthwork stands on a low hill on the left bank of the Avon, and seen from all sides has a noble and imposing outline. It contains an area of twenty-seven acres, enclosed by two great double banks and an immense ditch a mile in circumference. Both the plan and the situation of the fortress resemble the hill camps commonly supposed to belong to Neolithic times, though, as they now exist, the banks and ditches are smoother and more regular than is usual in these old earthworks. In the centre of the enclosure is a large mound, where recent investigations have disclosed masses of Norman masonry, and along the outer banks are fragments of huge stone walls. On the level turf between the ramparts and the keep, the outline of the Cathedral and other buildings can still be traced.

To the Romans Sarum was known as Sorbiodunum, or " dry city," and was evidently a very important station, with five great roads radiating from it to all points of the compass. Near by in the valley of the Avon, Cimric the Saxon, in 552 A.D. defeated the British Army and captured the fortress. Three hundred years later it was occupied by the Danes until driven out by Alfred, and in 960 A.D. Edgar held a Parliament here. On the Plains below, William the Norman reviewed

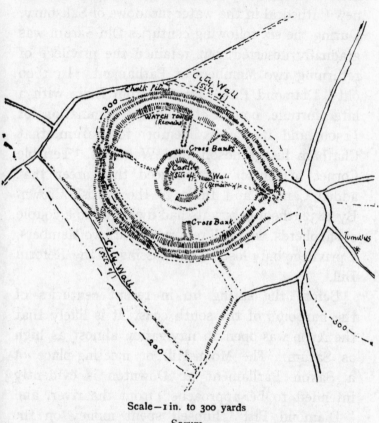

Scale—1 in. to 300 yards
Sarum

his army after the conquest of the country, " making all both great and small " take the Oath of Allegiance, before dismissing them to the lands he had given them. Then began the building of the great keep on the central mound, and the

Cathedral on the north front. But in such close quarters, priests and soldiers could not agree, and in 1220 the Bishop deserted the fort, and built a new Cathedral in the water meadows of Salisbury. During the six following centuries Old Sarum was gradually deserted, but retained the privilege of returning two Members of Parliament. In 1690 old " Diamond Pitt " retiring from India with a large fortune, bought the right of nomination for £1500, and it was as Member for Sarum, that Chatham his grandson, and Walpole's " Terrible Cornet of Horse " commenced the career that added Canada and India to the British Crown. By 1832, the inhabitants had dwindled to a couple of shepherds, who still returned their two Members, a privilege only lost by the passing of the Reform Bill.

Before the silting up in recent centuries of the harbours of the south coast, it is likely that the Avon was open to navigation almost as high as Sarum. The Moot Hill or meeting-place of a Saxon Parliament at Downton is evidently intended to be approached from the river, and " Diamond Pitt " himself spent money on the harbour at Christchurch, with the intention of making Salisbury a seaport. The position of Sarum may, therefore, have been selected in Neolithic times for its connection with the sea, and its convenience as a centre of distribution. Its importance may be gathered from the large number of great travel-ways that spread from it to all parts of the kingdom, which travel-ways the Romans afterwards converted into military roads, running to Winchester, Silchester, the Mendips, Blandford, and Badbury.

The land surrounding Old Sarum is full of Tumuli tumuli, ditches, and earthworks. The tumuli occupy many of the spurs of down between the Avon and the Bourne, the more important being found above the river fords, or at the meeting of the track-ways. A long barrow, hidden in trees, is placed at the point of land between the Avon and Nine Mile Brook, and has three round tumuli close by. Gallows Barrow, higher up the Avon, is on the line of a green road from Sidbury to Knighton Long Barrow, and Twin Barrow faces the single tumulus above Enford. On the hills forming the boundary of the plain to the north are a great number of round barrows, and long barrows are found on Fairmile Down, Wexcombe Down and Milton Hill, the last being known as the " Giant's Grave."

Ogbury is a large enclosure four miles north of Earthworks Sarum, and may possibly have served as a cattle —Ogbury compound to that fortress. It is surrounded by a single bank containing thirty-two acres, and there is a group of tumuli to the south, commanding easy access to the water at Durnford.

Two more earthworks, Chisenbury, and Lid- Lidbury and bury, lying on the line of the green road from Chisenbury

Inkpen, stand on the downs in the bend of the Avon as it turns south from Pewsey Valley. They may possibly, with Casterley Camp on the opposite bank, have served as resting-places after the passage of the river.

From Old Sarum the ancient ridge road to the

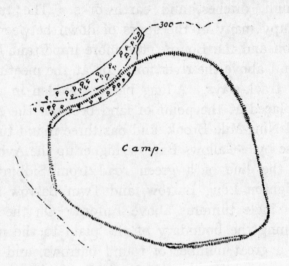

Scale—1 in. to 300 yards

Ogbury

north runs over Beacon Hill, and Sidbury Hill, to Easton Hill, a ditch following the trail for its whole length, with tumuli occupying nearly all the higher points. The road passes two transverse ditches that cross Beacon Hill on its northern and southern slopes, probably marking old trails running in the same direction. There are large groups of tumuli to the south of Beacon Hill, while at the foot of Sidbury is a circle of nine tumuli, one of which is saucer shaped.

On the northern slope of Sidbury Hill an important earthwork commands a wide extent of country. It is enclosed by double banks and ditches a mile in length, the outer bank being smaller than the inner. Within the camp is an ancient dew-pond that has never been known to run dry.

Sidbury Camp

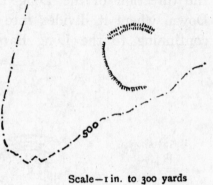

Scale—1 in. to 300 yards

Chisenbury Camp

Beyond Sidbury the old track-way continues along the ridge to Everley, passing many tumuli, and on Summer Down gives off a branch on the right to Fairmile Down, and another on the left to Pewsey Hill, the central trail joining the green road from Inkpen on Easton Hill. Numerous pack-trails are deeply bitten into the sides of Easton Hill, and it seems to have been the junction of many ways, from Chisbury, Fosbury, Sidbury, and Broadbury. The con-

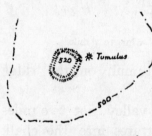

Scale—1 in. to 300 yards

Lidbury Camp

tinuation of the green road to Inkpen Beacon possibly followed the slightly lower ground by Grafton and Wexcombe Downs, but a trail also crosses the source of the Bourne at Aughton in the direction of the Long Barrow on Fairmile Down, where it divides into two branches, one continuing to the Long Barrow on Wexcombe

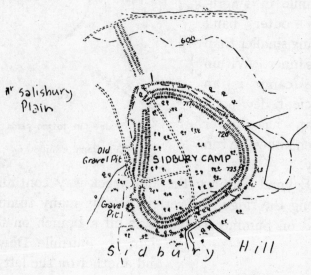

Scale—6 ins. to 1 mile

Down, the other to the tumuli on the ridge leading to Chute Causeway.

Plans of Valley

From Wexcombe Down a valley, not two miles wide at its entrance, penetrates into the chalk hills, a green road doubling back along its edge, and returning on the opposite side to Botley Hill. In dry weather this long detour could hardly have been necessary, and possibly the tumulus in the village of Marten may indicate a short cut to Botley Hill, while there is a second choice of roads by the ridge crossing the valley at Tidcombe. From Fosbury Valley an easy descent is made to the watershed of the Kennet and the Avon, offering the only opportunity of making the journey north without having to negotiate the muddy valleys of the Thames and Kennet. When watersheds were the only practical lines of travel, Fosbury must have been a busy station on the great north road, and a proof of its importance is revealed by traces of old terracings, ancient paths, ditches of defence, and a strong camp on the downs above. The Romans themselves were not blind to its advantages, and ran their road from Winchester to Cirencester down the valley, no doubt finding it dryer going than from Silchester across the Kennet mud to Speen.

The great camp of Fosbury, situated on an isolated plateau of down at the head of the valley, is defended by double lines of unusually high banks, with a deep ditch between, the whole measuring about three-quarters of a mile in circumference. *Fosbury Camp*

Except for the neck of land joining it with Haydown Hill, the position of the earthwork is entirely surrounded by a deep valley, terminating in the secluded and sheltered dell of Hippenscombe. At the connection with Haydown Hill is a group of small hollows, marked " chalk pits " on the maps, but which are more likely to have been pit dwellings serving as an outer guard to the camp. From this point a green road of great interest extends along the western side of the valley to the extreme point of Wexcombe Down, passing on its way two dry dew-ponds, and accompanied by a well-marked bank and ditch. At

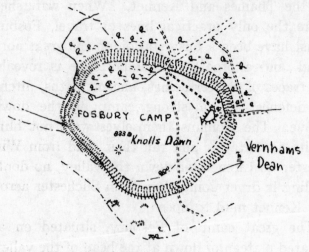

FOSBURY CAMP

833 Knolls Down

Vernhams Dean

Scale—6 ins. to 1 mile

the junction with the ridge from Tidcombe is a long barrow, that has been very thoroughly opened, and a little beyond are a pair of small twin barrows. From this point also a deep ditch runs at right angles across the valley, and a second transverse ditch is carried over the ridge, both probably forming outer defences to the camp. On Wexcombe Down are three tumuli, the most western having the appearance of a mutilated

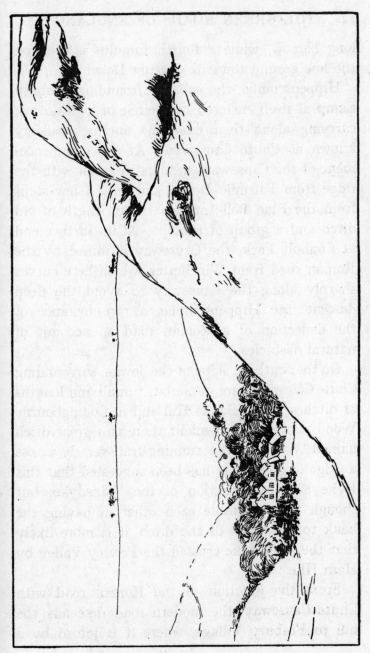

FOSBURY CAMP, HIPPENSCOMBE, AND CHUTE CAUSEWAY

long barrow, while a fourth tumulus is seen on the low ground towards Grafton Down.

Hippenscombe, the valley surrounding Fosbury Camp, is itself enclosed by a circle of high downs, carrying along their edge the ancient roadway known as Chute Causeway. At the commencement of the Causeway, near its junction with the ridge from Fairmile Down, and only a few steps from the Blue Bell Inn, is a short length of old ditch and a group of tumuli. At its further end at Conholt Park, the Causeway is joined by the Roman road from Winchester, which here curves sharply along the Causeway to avoid the deep descent into Hippenscombe, a rare instance of the deflection of a Roman road on account of natural obstacles.

On the southern slope of the downs, surrounding Chute Causeway, are numerous tumuli and lengths of ditches, as on Banks Hill and in Collingbourne Wood, while at Linkenholt there is a great ditch named Woden's Dyke, running transversely across a ridge of down. It has been suggested that this Dyke is a continuation of the Wansdyke, but though they resemble each other in having the bank to the south of the ditch, it is more likely that the Wansdyke crossed the Pewsey Valley by Ham Hill.

From the junction of the Roman road with Chute Causeway, the modern road descends the hill to Fosbury Village, where it is joined by a trail from the camp above, and completes the circle of the valley as a green road between Oxenwood and Botley Hill. Above Fosbury village a second trail probably followed the ridge, marked by two tumuli, that branches off on the right to Rivar Down, with the modern road to Hungerford running at its foot. The sides of Botley Hill are marked with many pack-trails worn smooth with much cultivation. They are shown as " Entrenchments " on the map, but entrenchments would probably encircle the hill, whilst these trails ascend it in the direction of a tumulus on the summit.

From Botley Hill the green ridge road is followed for miles over Botley Down and Rivar Down, by one of those lengths of ditches that so constantly accompany the old trackways. What purpose they served it is difficult to understand, unless they were intended to help travellers to put up a defence against sudden attack. On the other hand they were possibly formed by the hoofs of animals travelling in single file, and always following in the same line. From the tumulus on the crest of Rivar Down a good view is obtained of Chisbury Camp on the other side of Pewsey Valley, the fortress that guards the watershed on the north, as Fosbury defends it on the south. The Wansdyke in the present day, ends at the bottom of Chisbury Lane, where further traces of it are lost in the cultivated land. But there are many lengths of ditches on the downs south of the Kennet, that might easily have been continuations of the Dyke, perhaps the most likely being the bank and ditch by the roadside on Ham Hill.

Chisbury Camp

Chisbury Camp contains fifteen acres enclosed by double and triple ramparts. The modern road divides the camp into two sections, the eastern

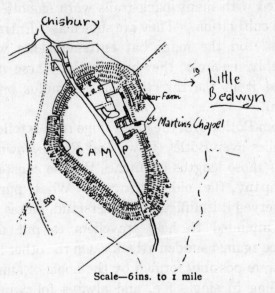

Scale—6 ins. to 1 mile

half being occupied by farm buildings and the ruins of the ancient chapel of St Martin; on the western side the banks are now mostly hidden by trees.

Beyond the tumulus on Rivar Down is a cutting in a beech wood, and looking down the opening it is seen to be continuous with an avenue in the woods beyond Bedwyn, where it joins the Roman road as it enters Savernake Park. On Ham Hill the trail crosses a well-marked bank and ditch, which as has been said already, may possibly be the continuation of the Wansdyke. Then passing two tumuli near the county boundary, the trail

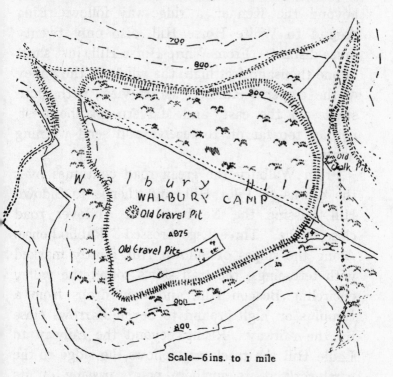

Scale—6 ins. to 1 mile

follows the ridge over Gallows Hill, and Inkpen Beacon, to Walbury Camp.

Walbury Camp, nine hundred and ninety-seven Walbury Camp feet above the sea-level, is situated on the northern-most curve of the chalk hills, south of the Kennet, and is enclosed within a single bank and ditch about a mile in circumference. The situation must have been singularly well chosen for beacon fires, as Winchester, which could be approached from the sea, is only twenty miles to the south with sloping ground all the way, whilst to the north beyond the Kennet, a ridge-way follows rising ground to White Horse Hill, also only twenty miles distant. From White Horse Hill, just short of one thousand feet high, the whole of the valley of the Upper Thames is within view, with Dunstable on the east, and Malvern on the west, neither too far off to receive and send warning lights.

From Walbury the green road continues over the downs to Pilot Hill, and thence to Sidown Hill, passing the Newbury and Andover road close to the " Three Legs Crossed " Public-house. Along the slopes of Sidown Hill, faintly marked with terracings, the trail skirts round the valley encircling Beacon Hill, and then drops from a tumulus on high ground to Seven Barrows close by the railway. Rising beyond the railway to Ladle Hill the track-way follows the ridge to the earthwork at its northern point, passing on its way a tumulus and a small Roman camp.

Beacon Hill and Ladle Hill Camps   Ladle Hill Camp, and the larger camp crowning Beacon Hill, must have formed an admirable defence to the pass into the chalk hills, where the railway now runs. Beacon Hill is a specially strong position, only to be approached by the

BEACON HILL FROM SEVEN BARROWS

steep hill-sides. The camp is defended by ramparts half a mile in circumference, slightly hour-glass in shape, and enclosing the summit of the hill almost exactly on the eight hundred foot contour.

Ladle Hill Camp is circular in form, with a tumulus close outside the bank. It is much smaller than Beacon Hill, and stands at the point

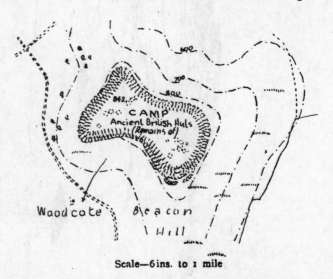

Scale—6ins. to 1 mile

of the hill overlooking the little valley that breaks the line of chalk downs. The green trail here follows along the ridge, passing half a dozen tumuli around Sydmonton Park, and continues beyond two groups of tumuli, in the direction of White Hill, and King John's Hill, to Plantation Hill. The Roman Port Way, on its road to Silchester, crosses the trail near a small and well-preserved Roman fort behind Woodgarston Farm, where a beautiful view is obtained over Silchester, and the low land spreading away to the Thames.

From Plantation Hill the ancient track-way is lost in a network of modern roads, but probably descended from Hannington to the watershed of the Test and Loddon, somewhere between the villages of Deane and Worting.

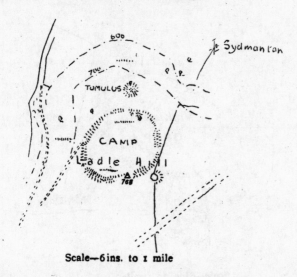

Scale—6 ins. to 1 mile

Winklebury Camp a little off the line of route is a single-banked enclosure, without any trace of the ditch remaining. Its situation on the slope of the hill does not appear to have been intended for defence.

The number of tumuli that existed until recently between the Loddon and the Test, may perhaps indicate the line taken by the ridge road from Inkpen, across the watershed. From Clarken

Green the old road, after joining the Harrow Way, would have followed the ground rising to the tumuli at Bull Bushes Copse, and passing a tumulus at Kempshott House, have led direct to Ellisfield Camp. From the junction of the Whitchurch and Winchester Railway, a second line of three tumuli can be traced over Battle

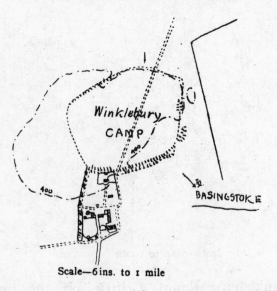

Scale—6 ins. to 1 mile

Down, to the ridge leading to Ellisfield through Farleigh Wallop.

Ellisfield Camp

Ellisfield is a fine specimen of a rectangular camp, enclosed by a single bank and ditch of unusual construction. The north, west, and south sides are gently bent inwards, with all four corners made higher than the rest of the bank. It is rare to find a rectangular camp on a hill-top, where a

circular contour fort might be expected. Perhaps
the importance of the situation as the meeting-
place of the roads from Inkpen, the Harrow Way,
and the road from Popham Beacon, may account
for its being altered and kept up to date, by those
who succeeded the men of the Stone Age.

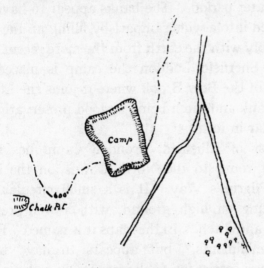

Scale—1 in. to 300 yards

Ellisfield Camp

The break in the chalk downs near Basingstoke
leaves the watershed of the Loddon and the Test
more open to attack than any point in the line
of hills from Wiltshire to Surrey, and the weakness
of the position has been defended by camps at
Old Basing and Sherfield Loddon and also perhaps
by the pre-Roman camp at Silchester, not two miles
distant. All three are placed on low ground, and

there must have been something unusual to account for circular forts occupying such a situation.

Old Basing In the garden of Old Basing House can still be traced the smooth and levelled outline of a ditch and two banks, and in the fields there are indications of earlier earthworks among the fortifications of a later period. The banks appear to have been formed into a wide rampart by filling up the ditch, possibly with the earth from the more recent moat.

Sherfield Loddon Camp At Sherfield Loddon the camp is placed in a bend of the Bow Brook where it joins the Loddon, the bank and ditch being in good preservation and circular in form.

East of Ellisfield, Crondall Camp lies in the direct route to the North Downs, on the line of the Pilgrim's Way. It is a small circular camp standing on high ground, with a well-preserved bank and ditch. In the maps it is named " Roman Entrenchments," but appears to have been a Norman castle, for ashlar stones have been found within its banks, and a valuable collection of Merovingian coins were unearthed here in 1828.

From Ellisfield twelve miles of hills stretch south to Old Winchester and Butser Hills, forming a connecting link between the North and South Downs. Butser Hill at the southern end of the link may be considered the commencement of the South Downs, and from it a line of forts stretch along the coast, as if to serve as a protection from sea enemies.

At Selbourne, about mid-distance between
Butser and Ellisfield, the chain of hills is
joined by the southern watershed, running
through Hindhead, Leith Hill, Crowborough
Beacon, and past Lymphe—the old landing-place

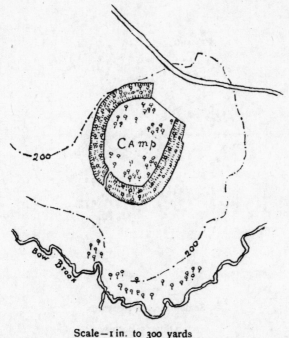

Scale—1 in. to 300 yards

Sherfield Loddon

overlooking Romney Marsh,—to terminate at
Cæsar's Camp above Folkestone. In early days
these hills were covered by the Andreada Forest,
which may account for there being fewer earthworks than is usual on so important a watershed.

At the union of the watershed with the hills stands a large camp, now known by the name of Oliver's Battery, perhaps in imitation of Oliver's Battery overlooking Winchester. It must at one time have been an important hill fortress, with

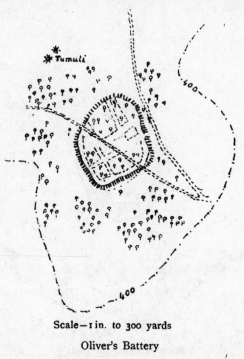

Scale—1 in. to 300 yards

Oliver's Battery

old trackways communicating north, south, east, and west, and with banks about a mile in circumference, though here and there the rampart and ditch are now almost lost in the hill-side. The site is beautiful with yews and gorse, and the camp is alive with rabbits, which are unfortunately slowly and surely destroying its banks.

CHAPTER VII

FOUR HAMPSHIRE ROADS

"For the wide green silence, and the moss-grown ways."

WITHIN the semicircle of hills that enclose Northern Hampshire, from Sarum to Inkpen, and Inkpen to Butser, four lines of communication follow ridges of high ground from east to west. Roman roads also intersect each other about the centre of the area, one running from Sarum to Silchester, the other from Winchester to Fosbury; while a third from Sarum to Winchester, completes the boundary to the south. This last Roman road crosses the Bourne from Old Sarum to Figsbury Camp,— named also Chlorus' Camp,—after a general of Dioclesian, who was Governor of Britain in 297 A.D. It is a small earthwork about four acres in extent, enclosed by a single bank, with an unusual inner ditch surrounding the central space. The Roman road from Figsbury can be clearly traced across the downs, with little hollows on either side from which the chalk has been removed to form its raised surface. After crossing the Test at Horsebridge, the road rises to a beautiful and secluded stretch of country over Ashley and Pitt Downs.

Figsbury Camp

To Winchester and Buster

137

On the highest point of Pitt Down there is a tumulus, visible from many miles around, which has been desecrated by a monument to a horse, that jumped into a chalk pit with his rider, without injury to either. Before coming to the tumulus a perfect little Roman camp is seen nestling in the valley to the north, with a bank connecting it with the hill above. In the village of Ashley on the far side of the hill, is a second small fort, perhaps an outpost of the larger camp in the valley.

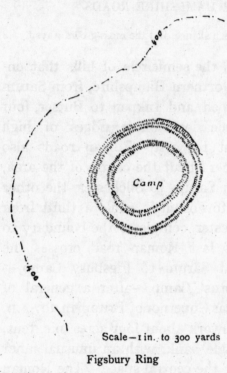

Scale—1 in. to 300 yards

Figsbury Ring

Beyond the southern slopes

Merdon Castle

of Pitt Down in the grounds of Hursley Park, the ramparts of Merdon Castle are still clear and distinct, though difficult to approach without permission from the owner. It is said that Cynewulf the Saxon king was murdered there in 755 A.D., when on a visit to his mistress, by the brother of the deposed Sigbert. It was here also that occurred the bloody slaughter of the Ethelwolf's army by the Danes in 867 A.D. The Norman castle of which the ruins still remain, was built in 1138 by Henry de Blois, Bishop of Winchester, brother of Stephen, and continued in the possession of the See of Winchester till Henry VIII's reign. In later times Merdon was the favourite home of Cromwell's son, "Tumbledown Dick," whose family appear to have been similarly attached to it, for after his exile, he was only able to recover possession by bringing an action at law against his daughters. In the last century Keble held the living, and loved the surrounding country.

From Pitt Down the Roman road is distinctly marked through woods and fields along the hillside, until after passing the golf links it descends into Winchester. It must have been along this road that Arthur and his knights journeyed from Winchester to the stations of the Round Table at Camelot and Caerleon, entitling it to be named the "Old Royal Road of England."

Forming a slight curve to the north of the straight Roman road, is a line of hills carrying many signs of ancient travel. Lobscombe Corner is scored with pack-trails, on Whitesheet Hill the road is deeply cut into the hill-side, and many tumuli stand above Buckholt. From Lobscombe Corner can be seen Wintersloe Hut, now the Pheasant Inn, where Hazlitt lived for a time, and

where the two volumes of his " Life of Napoleon "
were for the most part written. On the rising
ground behind the Hut are many large tumuli
and ancient banks, though now much over-run
with rabbits. Beyond the Test the trail takes
the high ground through the village of Ashley,

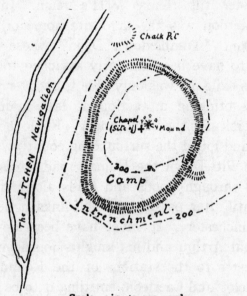

Scale—1 in. to 300 yards

St Catherine's Hill Camp

and following the hills where the Roman road now
runs, crosses the Itchen at Winchester.

Beyond Winchester the five tumuli on St Giles'
Hill probably indicate the direction of the track-
way on its ascent from the valley, and is there
joined by a short ridge from St Catherine's Hill
Camp. St Catherine's Camp consists of a single

bank and ditch about a mile in length, that encircles the summit of the hill, and is strongly defended for the whole of its circumference by the steep slopes of the down. From Five Barrows the trail probably kept the line of the modern road, which follows the high ground for some eight miles to Beacon Hill, standing opposite Old Winchester Hill, on the other side of Meon

Old Winchester Hill and Camp

Valley. Old Winchester Hall carries a camp on its summit very similar in position and design to St Catherine's Camp. It too is enclosed by a single bank and ditch, while trails ascend to it up the easier slopes of the hill from north and south, and a green road runs east along the ridge to Butser Hill, where it becomes continuous with the trail along the South Downs.

From Figsbury or Chlorus' Camp, a second

green road runs along the line of hills, parallel to the river Bourne, as far north as Fosbury. Quarley Hill is passed on the right, a landmark difficult to escape in these parts of Hampshire, as its summit surrounded with a single bank and ditch, and crowned with a clump of trees, is never possible to mistake. Close at hand it is difficult to realize that its gentle slopes should stand out so distinctly

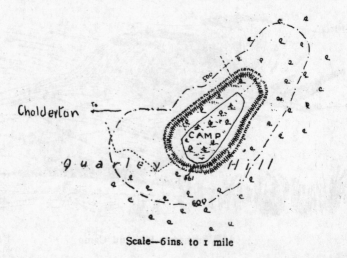

Scale—6 ins. to 1 mile

when seen from distant uplands, where Quarley often proves useful in giving the direction of track-ways, and is as welcome to the view as Fuji to the Japanese.

On the southern foot of the hill the Roman road from Sarum passes on its way to Silchester, and from near Grateley railway station a green road runs south-east along the ridge to Danebury. This magnificently imposing fortress rivals Old

Sarum itself, its square, sullen, and beetling outline looking the very picture of a savage stronghold. It is defended by three tiers of ramparts,
and an elaborately defended entrance. The
surrounding downs are crowded with many tumuli,

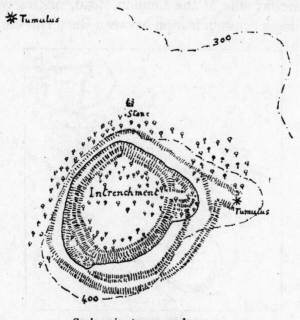

Scale—1 in. to 300 yards

Danebury

while a group of seven barrows below Chattis Hill,
mark the graves of warriors who may have either
stormed or defended the earthwork.

Four miles across the downs to the north of **Bury Hill**
Danebury, Bury Hill and Balksbury Camps stand **Camp**
on opposite hills, with the Little Ann flowing in
the valley between,—one of the many instances

of the close association of a more strongly defended camp with a single banked enclosure. Beyond Clatford, at the foot of Bury Hill, a green trackway known as the Ladies Walk, circles round Bere Hill to the south of Andover, and joins the Ox Drove on the far side of the London Road, in this way forming a communication between Bury Hill Camp

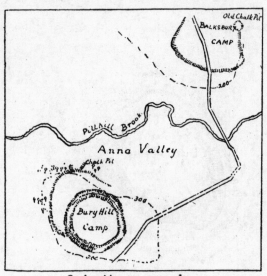

Scale—½ in. to 300 yards

and the ancient Harrow Way. In these chalk districts the old travel ways do not avoid crossing the rivers with the exaggerated horror that is universal in the clay country. Instead of a muddy bottom, a good paving of flints must have remained in the river bed after the chalk had been washed away, giving as firm a footing for packhorses as the open down itself.

On the opposite side of the Test to Danebury,
Stockbridge Down is capped by Woolbury Ring,
an enclosure about four acres in extent, surrounded
by a single bank and ditch. It is remarkable how
often the important earthworks have such enclosures in more or less close proximity, and not

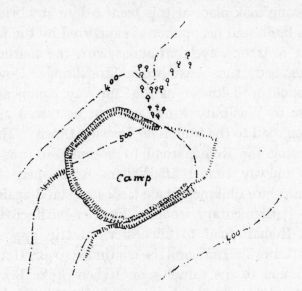

Scale—1 in to 300 yards

Woolbury Ring

infrequently separated by a river, as at Badbury
and Spettisbury, Bury Hill and Balksbury,
Yarnbury and Codford, Sarum and Ogbury,
Totternhoe and The Maiden near Dunstable, and
Battlesbury and Scratchbury at Warminster. No
one, who has had experience of ranching, can think
it possible that men and cattle could have inhabited

the same enclosure, and it may be an allowable conjecture that these secondary rings served as cattle compounds for the garrisons in the larger forts.

The Lun Way The double name of Stock-Bridge suggests, as Mr Shaw has pointed out, that an important crossing took place at this point before any bridge was built, and his opinion is supported by the fact that a track-way, continuous with the southern watershed, runs east from Stockbridge Down. This old trail, known as the Lun Way, commences close to Woolbury Ring, and can be traced as a green road to the tumuli on Crawley Down. Then crossing the Roman road to Fosbury, it runs to the railway tunnel at Wallers Ash, where the Hampshire Clubmen made their last stand against the Parliamentary troops. Further on it crosses the Roman road to Silchester, exactly opposite the Lunway Inn, and is continued over Itchen Common to the tumulus on Itchen Stoke Down, when after crossing the river at the Mill Ford, it arrives at Oliver's Battery on the heights of Abbotstone. The words " Lun," " Lud," " Lad," " Lidd," and " Lyd " occur frequently in the course of the old travel-ways, as the Lyddway in Pewsey Valley, the many Lydiards on the water-shed north of Avebury, Liddington on the Icknield Way, Lad Barrow in Oxfordshire, and Ladbrook and Ludgate in London. It has been explained that the derivation of these names is from the

Saxon word "Leodi," meaning public or popular, and therefore especially appropriate to frequented roads.

The modern road from Stockbridge follows a ridge of down a little north of the Lunway, leading to a group of tumuli near the Roman road, and then stretches away for ten miles to Popham Beacon, where there are five tumuli arranged in a line from north to south. It passes midway between Norsbury Camp, above Stoke Charity, and Tidbury Camp near Bullington. Little remains of Norsbury save its single bank and ditch,

Norsbury, Tidbury, and the Andyke

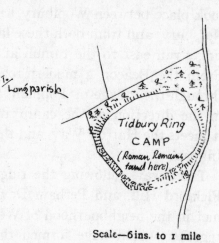

Scale—6 ins. to 1 mile

but Tidbury is in a better state of preservation, and was evidently of much greater consequence. At Bransbury a considerable bank and ditch, known as the Andyke, runs between the Test and the Andover Road, but it can hardly have been a defence against the river, as the ditch is on the higher ground. More likely it formed one of the sides of a rectangular camp, and owed its preservation to the roadway running along its front, while the rest of the camp has been ploughed out. A mile away, at Barton Stacey in the fields at the back of the Manor Farm, a large Roman Camp can be traced above the river bank.

No sign of the old trackway from Stockbridge to Popham can now be found, unless it may be by the lines of yews that flourish on the hill sides. But there can be little doubt that communication took place between Woolbury Ring, Tidbury, and Norsbury, and from both these latter camps slight ridges run east to the tumuli at Popham Beacon. From the Beacon a modern road follows a ridge through the village of Popham, and rises steadily in the direction of the camp at Ellisfield, where it meets the Harrow Way, and the green road from Inkpen.

The Harrow Way Track-ways following the ridges from Quarley, Pickford Hill, and Perham Down, must all have met in the neighbourhood of Weyhill, and joining together would have formed the commencement of the Harrow Way, which Dr Stevens points out in his History of St Mary Bourne, is mentioned in a Saxon Charter of the date 900 A.D., as the Hoare or Ancient Way. Its first length of about a mile and a half runs from Weyhill almost to the river Anton, and it might have been supposed that this most ancient highway would have been preserved with scrupulous care, but unfortunately a portion of it has been enclosed as a cottager's garden.

Beyond the river a modern road continues, in

the same direction as this first stretch of the Harrow Way, to a ridge of high ground leading to the Test. Where the road mounts the hill it is joined by the Ox Drove coming from the Ladies Walk and Bury Hill Camp. A little further, at the highest point of the down, it passes the Devil's Dyke, which has been cut through by the railway, and now forms the boundary of a small wood. Near by a Roman station is said to have stood on the line of the road to Silchester. After passing Apsley Farm the road drops to the valley of the Test, and crosses the river at Chapman's Ford. The ford also seems to have been the meeting-place of a road from Danebury, as above Apsley a field path known as the Old Road can be followed along the ridge skirting Harewood Forest, to Goodworth Clatford, Barrow Hill, Rowbury, and the Danebury entrenchments. From Chapman's or the Pedlar's Ford the road continues beyond Hurstborne Station, and passing under a single railway arch, mounts to Lark Barrow Hill, where it is again locally spoken of as the Harrow Way. On the high ground two miles north of the railway **Egbury** is situated Egbury Camp, with wide and extensive **Camp** outlook, and has the appearance of being a contour fort altered and adapted by the Romans. From Lark Barrow Hill the Harrow Way becomes a clearly marked green road running parallel to the railway, the worn slopes of its undulations, and its numerous old thorns, junipers, and yews

stamping it with the seal of antiquity. The old
road probably turned a little south at Clarken
Green to round the head waters of the Test, and
after crossing the watershed, mounted the rising

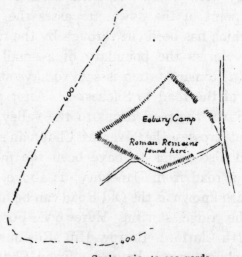

Eobury Camp

Roman Remains
found here.

Scale—1 in. to 300 yards

ground to Ellisfield Camp. There, meeting with
trails from Inkpen and Popham Beacon, the
united roads continued their course along the
North Downs, following much the same direction
as that taken in later days by the Pilgrims Way.

CHAPTER VIII

AVEBURY TO STREATLEY

"The owld White Horse wants zettin to rights,
And the Squire hev promised good cheer,
Zo we'll gie un a scrape to kip un in zhape,
And a'll last for many a year."

IN the first chapter the Ridgeway was traced *The Ridgeway* over Hackpen Hill to Barbury Camp, where it descends by Gipsy Lane to the watershed at the head of the Og Valley. The modern road runs on a slightly lower level than the old course, which follows the line of three tumuli standing on the watershed, and after crossing the Roman road from Fosbury, mounts the ascent to Liddington Castle. This earthwork faces Barbury on the opposite side of the valley, the two fortresses keeping guard over the entrance into the Down country. From Liddington the Ridgeway runs as a broad green road for more than thirty miles to the Thames at Streatley. It follows the escarpment of the chalk a little below the sky line, the road varying from 600 feet to 900 feet in height, the air is bright and bracing, and all the way under foot spreads soft and springy turf. There are no special boundaries, except, here and there, banks thrown up at the time of the enclosures, but the course is clearly marked by the darker and finer turf that comes from much trampling, and in the springtime by the multitude of daisies that grow in the closer soil. A spreading view of middle England stretches away to the north, with the Thames in the near distance, and it is said that on clear days the smoke of Birmingham can be seen, more than a hundred miles away. The whole length of the road is practically an undisputed solitude, for hardly a dozen people will be met with, unless it is a string of racehorses out for exercise with their lads. Large earthworks stand along its course at fairly regular intervals, pack-trails are worn on the slopes of its undulations, and solitary tumuli are found at the junctions of the smaller ridgeways. The road is planned on a not unskilful strategy, connecting the eastern and western watersheds. The earthworks must have been erected at the expense of much labour and are designed on similar principles. All this cannot have been the work of local tribes at war with each other, but clearly suggests that the country, when the road was made, was ruled by a common authority, exercising at least a loose control over the territories through which it ran. If the earthworks, as by common consent date to the Stone Age, then the Ridgeway belongs to the same period, and is proof of a civilization existing in this country much earlier than has been suspected. In China and the East there were no doubt older

LIDDINGTON CASTLE

roads, but most of these have been buried in sand, whilst the kindly turf of our climate has formed a protecting covering to the Ridgeway, till now perhaps it can claim to be actually the oldest road in the world.

Below the slope of the chalk cliffs a second road known as the Port Way, runs parallel to the Ridgeway above. This road was known in Saxon times as the Icknield Way, and it is only since the eighteenth century that its name has been applied to the Ridgeway. The Port Way has no resemblance to a Roman road, and may with more likelihood be attributed to the Bronze Age. As the land became better settled, it was possible to avoid the greater exposure of the hilltops, and by following the line of springs, water would be more abundant, whilst with the introduction of wheeled traffic there would be a constant tendency to keep to the valley levels.

Liddington Liddington Castle, which can be marked from afar by its bleak little group of fir trees, was the favourite haunt of Richard Jefferies, and here he lay on its banks, with his face to the sky, and prayed that he might become an angel before his time. It was known in former days as Badbury, and has given its old name to a little village that lies at the foot of its northern front. Surrounding the camp are signs of extensive settlements, and these with the track-ways leading over the downs to the south, and the line of hills to Wroughton, mark it as a meeting-place from Bincknol, Barbury, Uffington, and Chisenbury and Sarum. From the south of the camp a beautiful grass road descends the ridge to the Kennett, crossing the river in much the same position as the railway, where

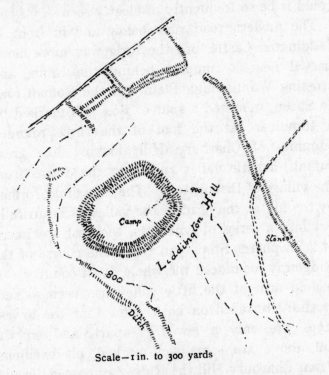

Scale—1 in. to 300 yards

ancient travel has scored the steep further bank with some dozen deep pack-trails. A branch trail is given off in the direction of the British village at Upper Upham, from which five tumuli lead to the village of Aldbourne. A further trail runs along the ridge of Sugar Hill to Four Burrows, as if making for the conspicuous tumulus on the downs above Baydon, indicating the way to Membury Camp. The position of this tumulus, like many others scattered over the downs, must have been very carefully chosen, for in no other situation could it be so frequently or clearly seen.

The modern road runs below and in front of Liddington Castle, but the Ridgeway more likely passed near a tumulus behind the camp, and crossing Wanborough Plain and the Roman road to Speen, mounted a spur of Fox Hill marked by a tumulus. At the foot of the three rounded summits of Charbury Hill, looking like great tumuli, a little valley runs into the downs from the village of Bishopstone. The semicircle, formed by the hill at the head of the valley, is beautifully cut into a series of lynchetts, the best specimens of " Shepherds Steps " in the whole course of the Ridgeway, or indeed the whole down country. A second arm of the little valley has been so successfully terraced on both sides that the lowest steps are only a few feet apart, and on the hill above are some well-marked pit-dwellings. From Charbury Hill the Ridgeway passes through cultivated country, and near the country boundary the ground is often heavy going. Pack-trails on the right mark a green road running in the direction of a tumulus on Hinton Down, and further on to the tumulus above Baydon. Looking back from the Ridgeway over Wanborough Plain, the view

Charbury
Hill

of Liddington with the sun setting behind it is
magnificent, the frowning outline of the hill
resembling an immense fortress dominating all
the land.

A copy, to the left of the Ridgeway, as it **Wayland**
mounts White Horse Hill, conceals Wayland **Smith's**
Smith's cave. It is probably the remains of a **Cave**
long barrow, the exposed stones forming part of

Lynchetts near Bishopstone

a central passage with chambers on either side.
The monument is mentioned by Sir Walter Scott
in Kenilworth, and Camden associates it with the
traditional invisible blacksmith, who for a piece
of silver replaced lost horse-shoes.

A mile further brings us to the top of White
Horse Hill, nine hundred and seventy-three feet
above the sea-level, and the northernmost point
of the chalk hills between Avebury and Streatley.

To obtain control of this central position must have been of supreme importance to invaders from the south. In front it commands the whole of the Upper Thames, whilst the Ridgeway gives easy access to the eastern and western watersheds. To the south Inkpen Beacon is less than twenty miles away, whilst Winchester and Southampton Water are little more than a day's journey from Inkpen, so that within two days of landing from the sea, an enemy might be in command of the very heart of the country, with a speedy and easy retreat in case of necessity. Or coming by Christchurch, and making their way up the Avon, they might reach White Horse Hill by way of Fosbury, without having to cross a single river.

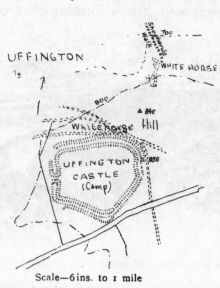

Scale—6 ins. to 1 mile

Uffington Camp and the White Horse

Uffington Castle stands on the flat plateau of the hill, defended by a formidable bank and ditch containing eight acres. Below the Castle on the right the famous White Horse is cut in the turf, and just below the horse's head Pendragon's Hill

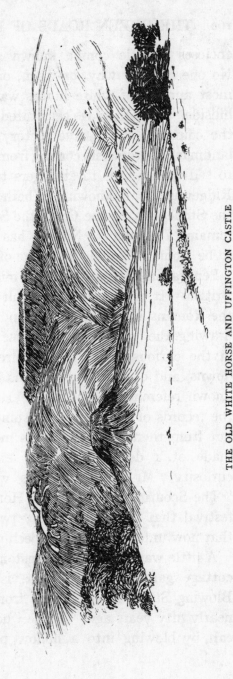

THE OLD WHITE HORSE AND UFFINGTON CASTLE

encloses a little combe known as the Manger. No one can say why, or when, or by whom, this most ancient of white horses was traced on the hillside. Whether it celebrated a conquest of the country, or a native victory, or served as a landmark to travellers coming from the low country to sell their wares to strangers travelling on the Ridgeway, is unknown. Whether it belongs to the Stone Age, to the Celts, the Saxons or Danes, remains a mystery. No one has ever thought it to be Roman, though the name of Arthur's father " Pendragon " suggests that it might be Romano-British. It is, however, difficult to believe that the Romans left behind them no greater skill in drawing the outlines of a horse than is shown in the curious and wan creature traced on the downs, and on the cover of this book. The first known reference to the White Horse is found in the records of the Abbey of Abingdon, 1471 A.D., but from then to recent times mention is hardly made of a device that now excites all men's curiosity. Mr Hughes in his well-known book " The Scouring of the White Horse " describes a festival that took place every twenty years, and that now unfortunately has been abandoned.

A little way down the Kingston Lisle road, in a cottage garden on the right, is the celebrated Blowing Stone, brought here from the Ridgeway nearly fifty years ago. Those who know the trick can, by blowing into a hollow, produce a sound like that of a foghorn, and it is seldom that one of the beautiful girls from the cottage is unwilling to instruct the stranger.

Below the western slope of White Horse Hill, in a wood above Compton Beauchamp, is an earthwork containing about five acres known as Hardwell Camp, and on the downs near Ashdown Park is a still smaller earthwork named King Alfred's Castle. It was on the heights of Ashdown, as already mentioned, that Alfred turned on the Danes, after his defeat at Reading, and gained the first of the victories that eventually freed Wessex from the invaders.

From Uffington Castle a green trail follows the **Lambourn** southern slope of White Horse Hill, past Idle Bush Barrow and the Hangman's Stone, to the little town of Lambourn, where Alfred's widow retired on the death of the King. The town lies in a saucer formed by the surrounding downs, and old trails radiate from it to camps at all points of the compass, Membury and Liddington to the west, Uffington and Hardwell to the north, Letcombe to the east, and Borough Hill and Bussocks Wood to the south. To the south also a Roman road follows the ridge from Speen, on its way to Cirencester. It was along this road that troops would have been sent to the Ridgeway, and making Lambourn their centre, could have been diverted to almost any point of the horizon.

Deep trails by the side of the road to Hungerford,

as it ascends Coppington Hill, make for the direction of Membury Camp, placed on the hill overlooking Marridge Down. It is about ten acres in extent, surrounded by a wood and enclosed with a well-preserved bank and ditch, which are covered in spring with primroses and wild hyacinths.

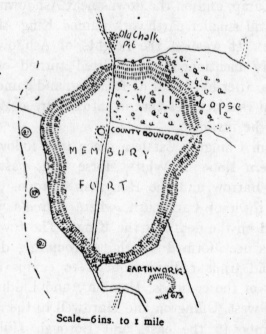

Scale—6 ins. to 1 mile

The camp is in communication with Liddington, by the trail running over Sugar Hill, and with Uffington, by the green road that passes the tumulus on the heights of Row Down. The camp, in fact, would seem to have served as a depôt for both fortresses.

The trail from Lambourn to Letcombe ascends

Ewe Hill, and crossing Nutwood Down by a tumulus, reaches the Ridgeway close to the camp. In the valley to the left of Ewe Hill are a collection of tumuli, known as Seven Barrows, though actually nineteen can still be counted. One of the barrows is surrounded by a bank and ditch, and the group is believed to be an ancient burial ground. At the foot of Ewe Hill a second trial is given off on the right to Wether's Barn, where a tumulus half way up the hill, marks the meeting-place of four green roads. One runs north, past a tumulus on Mere End Down, to the Ridgeway,—a second passing two tumuli at the foot of Woolley Down goes to Farnborough,—a third travelling over Kite Hill passes the Hangman's Stone, and goes to Borough Hill Camp, while the fourth reaches to the Lambourn River at East Garston.

Continuing along the Ridgeway from White Letcombe Horse Hill a tumulus is passed at the junction of the road from Lambourn. From this point Hackpen Hill, enclosing Crow Hill Bottom, juts out to the north, with two tumuli on its ridge with a group of pit dwellings at the point of the hill. A little more than three miles further, Letcombe Castle or Segsbury Camp is built on Castle Hill, above Wantage. It stands on the 700-foot contour, rather below the surrounding hills, and has an area of twenty-seven acres, enclosed by a not very formidable bank and ditch.

In the vallum to the south Dr Phine, in 1871, found a sarsen stone, covering a cist made of flints, and containing fragments of human bones, broken pieces of pottery, and flint scrapers. Below the hill on the right is Wantage Workhouse, where not long ago resided an ancient shepherd and local poet, who expressed his complete content now

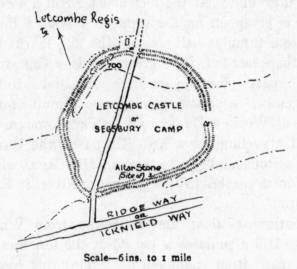

Scale—6 ins. to 1 mile

that he had " an armchair and a'ways an a'dience."

A little beyond Letcombe the course of the Ridgeway is crossed by the road to Hungerford, where a branch appears to have been given off to the valley, while close by are the only two houses met with in the whole course of the Ridgeway between Avebury and the Thames. A mile further a tumulus stands at the junction of a green road to Farnborough, and beyond, on

Betterton Down, three tumuli once stood. On one
of these has been erected a monument to a gallant
soldier, that certainly cannot justify the destruction of an ancient tumulus, and that as a record
of private affection is offensively conspicuous.
Near the green road to Farnborough, Grim's Ditch
coming from Lambourn Downs crosses the Ridge-

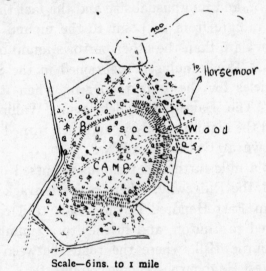

Scale—6 ins. to 1 mile

way, and follows it to the north for the rest
of its course as far as Lowbury Hill and
Aldworth.

Returning to the Ridgeway a green road **Bussocks Wood Camp**
branches off to the right near the reservoir, and can
be followed to Bussocks Wood Camp, passing the
Stanmore tumulus about half-way. A little distance further down the Ridgeway Cwichelmes **Cwichelmes Low**
Low is reached, standing in a copse to the

right. It is a large tumulus that measured, in Colt Hoare's time, four hundred feet round the base, and seventy-seven feet in height. Since then it has been badly excavated, and now its proportions are less than half of these dimensions. It is supposed to be named after Cwichelme, a king of the West Saxons who died in 686 A.D., and its unusual size and the fact that no roads radiate from it, point to the mound being of later date than the other barrows found on the downs. The tumulus is mentioned in the Saxon Chronicles for the year 1000 A.D., when it says that " The Danes after destroying Wallingford passed the night at Cholsey, and then turned along Ashdown at Cwichelmes Low."

Sinodun   Not a mile further, a tumulus is passed on the left of the Ridgeway, where a green track joins it from East Hendred Down. This trail can be followed to Chilton, and further to a tumulus on Hagbourne Hill, where the roads between East and West Hagbourne become complicated. But if the trail followed the highest ground, as is natural to suppose, it led directly to the earthwork of Sinodun, situated on the Thames just below Dorchester. As Wittenham Clumps, it is well known to boating men, and seems impossible to escape, since it keeps within view for miles of river rowing. As an outpost of the Ridgeway, no position could have been better chosen for guarding the river, and immediately opposite

where the Thame joins the Thames, the strip of
land between the two streams is defended by the
Devil's Dyke. From East Hendred Down, on the
south side of the Ridgeway, the trackway
runs to Old Down, where it is marked by many
pack-trails, and continues to Catmore and Stanmore
tumulus. There it divides into two branches,

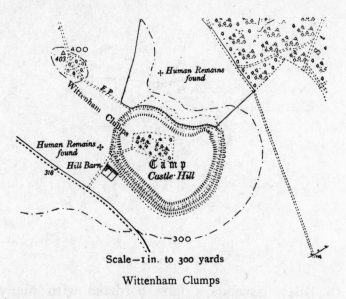

Scale—1 in. to 300 yards

Wittenham Clumps

one going to Bussocks Wood Camp near Chieveley,
and the other to Borough Hill Camp.

The Ridgeway from East Hendred Down inclines
a little south, and after crossing the Newbury and
Oxford road branches into three divisions. The
middle or main division continues along the high
ground to Roden Down, the trail overlooking Churn
Valley, with Grim's Ditch following on the left

for the whole distance.   Churn Valley is a favourite
ground during the summer for cavalry training,
when it is a strange contrast to see the three large
tumuli standing on the low ground among the
soldiers' tents.   The second branch of the Ridgeway runs south, over a beautiful stretch of turf
to the village of Compton, and crossing the road

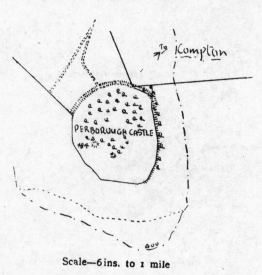

Scale—6 ins. to 1 mile

to Ilsley, ascends a lane bordered with many
Perborough pack-trails, to join beneath Perborough Camp a
Camp modern road named the West Ridgeway.   The
camp was evidently at one time of considerable strength, though its ramparts have suffered
much from the inroads of agriculture.   At
Hampstead Norris two tumuli stand on either
side the headwaters of the Pang, apparently
in the line of a trackway coming from Streatley,

and marking the shortest and driest way across the valley. The West Ridgeway follows the eastern boundary of the Berkshire Downs to the Kennett, Oareborough and Oare Hills being passed on the right, both carrying slight remains of earthworks. On the left just beyond Her- **Grimsbury Camp**
mitage railway station, and hidden in a wood,

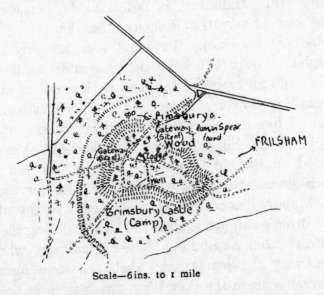

Scale—6 ins. to 1 mile

Grimsbury Camp completes the eastern defences of the downs. The banks are much decayed, but the entrance is remarkable for being defended by a long projecting bank. From Grimsbury a spur from the downs runs west, dividing the Kennett and the Pang, and a modern road follows its crest over Bucklebury Common, through a beautiful avenue of trees, to its extreme point, where there are slight indications of a small earthwork. Unfortunately an irate owner refused permission to make a careful examination of the ground.

There are indications that the third branch of the Ridgeway enclosed Churn Hill, and joined the main branch on Roden Down behind Low-bury Hill. Indeed it is not unlikely, considering how closely the Ridgeway has kept to the edge of the chalk, that this was its original course. Churn Hill has long been under cultivation, and all traces of the road itself are lost, but from Fox Barrow, at the head of Churn Valley, a line of five tumuli can be traced along the outer slope of the hill, and may be assumed to have stood on the old trackway. Blewburton Hill is seen immediately below, with its sides terraced with many lynchettes. It is believed to be the site of Alfred's ambush against the Danes, during their retreat from Aesundun. A few years ago, when repairing the road, many skeletons were found buried beneath the Port Way, and may have been the results of such an engagement. From Churn Hill the trail must have crossed Fairmile Bottom to the slopes of Lowbury Hill, to join again with the Ridgeway on Roden Down. On Lowbury the low banks of a square Roman camp can still be seen, and a tumulus stands just outside the ramparts. An abundant spring of water flows from the side of the hill, and over the floor of the camp many oyster shells are found, so that on the whole Lowbury appears to have offered fairly comfortable summer quarters for the hardy Roman soldier. Below the camp Fairmile itself runs as a broad stretch of green turf towards the nearest point of the Thames at Moulsford.

From Roden Down the Ridgeway drops abruptly into Streatley, where before reaching the old rectory, the green road gradually loses its turf, and then follows the modern road to the river. At Streatley the Thames is wide and shallow, with gently shelving banks, and before the narrowing of the channel cannot have been difficult to cross. But Streatley does not appear to have been the only place of crossing, as from the village of Compton deep pack-trails ascend Apple Pie Hill, and joining with a track-way from Roden Down, follows the modern road along the ridge to Pangbourne. The road passes the village of Aldworth, where the last is seen of Grim's Ditch, that has followed the Ridgeway continuously from Lambourn Downs. It is a likely situation for a contour fort, and slight evidences of an earthwork still remain, but are probably of later date. Aldworth was for centuries the seat of the de la Beche family, and lately Mrs Alexander has unravelled a wonderful romance from their records. It appears that Margery de la Beche (*née* Poyings) was a ward of King Edward III's, and by his order was married to Nicholas de

la Beche, the tutor of the Black Prince. Upon
his death at the castle of Aldworth in 1345, his
neighbour Gerard de Lisle obtained the King's
warrant to marry the widow, and a ceremony, both
forced and false, took place, for Gerard was already
married. John de Dalton, an old lover of Margery,
left her former home in Lincolnshire with thirty
knights and men-at-arms to release her, and was
joined by an equal number of Berkshire squires.
They stormed the castle, and leaving Sir Gerard
bound in the hall, set out for Scotland, with writs
and sheriffs at their heels in every county of
England. After three years of outlawry, the
rebels, one by one, joined His Majesty, then at war
in Gascony, and obtained pardon. John de Dalton
and Margery landed at Calais for the same purpose,
and there the lady died shortly before the King's
pardon arrived.

There are indications of trails leading from the
ridge to both Basildon and Pangbourne, the two
points where the chalk hills come nearest to those
on the opposite side of the river. From these
steep banks the passage must have been accomplished by rafts or coracles, possibly an easier task
in wet weather than struggling through the muddy
approaches of the ford at Streatley. When the
Ridgeway was first designed there may possibly
have been no river to cross, for the Berkshire Downs
were once connected with the Chiltern Hills, and the
Thames emptied itself into the Wash. The troubles

of crossing only began when the river had undermined the cliff, and broken through Goring Gap, to find an exit into the Kennett Valley.

In the low ground beneath the chalk downs, a _{The} slight ridge runs from Wootton Bassett to Oxford, passing through Highworth and Farringdon. This ridge is guarded by five earthworks, which besides offering shelter to travellers may have served as outposts of the Ridgeway, to keep watch over the Thames. Below Oxford we have already seen that Sinodun commands the river from Abingdon to Wallingford, and is in direct communication with the Ridgeway.

The camp west of Wootton Bassett at Bradenstoke-cum-Clack has already been mentioned in the chapter on Avebury. Ringsbury, the next camp, is situated above the village of Purton, and is doubly important, since not only is it a link in the chain of forts along the Farringdon Ridge, but also stands on the highest point of the watershed between the Thames and the Avon, forming the first station from Avebury on the route to the Cotswolds and the north. The camp is found behind a charming little Jacobean house at Restrop, and has a fine view over the country to the west. On Purton Common, a mile to the north, are further remains of banks and entrenchments. Of the third camp only an imperfect bank and ditch remain on Castle Hill above Broad Blunsden, but there are indications that the earthwork was once much more extensive. On high ground, to the west of Farringdon, a circular camp lies hidden in a wood, with its bank and ditch in good preservation, and to the south of the same high ground, near Little Coxwell, are extensive remains of a British village. Between Buckland and Kingston Bagpuze, lying off the road to the right,

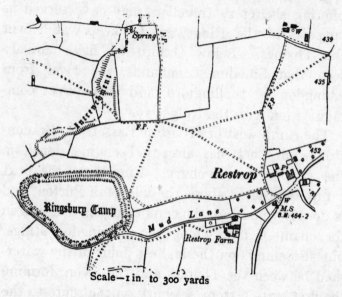

Scale—1 in. to 300 yards

Cherbury Camp is situated close to a little branch of the river Ock. It is circular in form, but stands rather off the ridge, and may have served perhaps as a cattle compound rather than as a work of defence. It is also claimed that Oxford Castle occupied the site of an ancient fort, but whether this is so or not, the ridge road must have forded the river close by, and, likely enough, was defended long before the Norman castle was erected.

By deserting the Ridgeway, and following the Farringdon Ridge, the journey from Avebury to the Chiltern Hills would be considerably shortened, and the difficulties of crossing the Thames would have been hardly greater at Oxford than at Streatley. If the line of the Farringdon Ridge is continued beyond Oxford, it is found to pass the earthworks near Brill and Bolbec, and to join the Icknield Way at Ivinghoe, on the watershed of the Ouse and the Thame.

CHAPTER IX

THE EASTERN WATERSHED

" To the wild woods and the downs—
To the silent wilderness,
Where the soul need not repress
Its music, lest it should not find
An echo in another's mind."

AFTER crossing the Thames at Streatley, the Icknield Way follows the western slope of the Chiltern Hills, occupying much the same relative position as the Port Way to the Berkshire Downs. The Chiltern Hills are no longer open downs, but closely cultivated, and it is now difficult to say if the Ridgeway once ran over the higher ground. The ridges stretch north-east to south-west, so that a road along the hill-tops must have crossed many little valleys, and the situation of the Icknield Way on the water-shed, would always have offered the more convenient route, for here the highest land does not form the dividing line between the rivers. Following the modern road from Goring to Cleeve, and there turning to the right, the first stretch of the Icknield Way is found at the foot of the hills. It runs as a green road for two miles past the village of Ipsden, and is then crossed by Grim's Ditch, clearly seen on either side. This ditch extends in Grim's Ditch a straight line from the Thames at Mongewell, over the Chilterns near Nutfield, and then again descends to the Thames at Henley. It keeps parallel to the Oxford and Henley road on the southern side, and forms a defence or boundary to the land enclosed by a long loop of the Thames on its other three sides. From Mongewell it is only a short distance across the Thames to Churn Hill, where it will be remembered there is another Grim's Ditch, that has come all the way from Lambourn Downs. If these two ditches were ever parts of a connected whole, they may have formed a boundary to a not unnatural division of territory. A third Grim's Ditch appears to have run along the Chilterns, its first length now being met with at Lacy Green on the north side of Bledlow Ridge, while separate lengths are found at Great Hampden, near the banks known as the Danish Camp, also at Hunis Hill, at Cock's Hill, on the downs above Wigginton, and on Berkhampstead Common. It is interesting to find remains of camps at Chartridge and Cholesbury, standing on the line taken by the ditch, whilst its last length seems to be making for the direction of the Audreys. This association of ditches and earthworks suggests that they may mark the line of a ridgeway north of the Thames, and from the hills above the river at Whitchurch to Bledlow Ridge, there are many lengths of modern road occupying positions where the ridgeway would naturally run. From Grim's Ditch, the Icknield Way circles round the hills to Swyncombe Down— where there are some banks known as Danish Entrenchments,—and leaving Watlington well on the left, approaches the railway under Beacon Hill. Opposite this point the Lower Icknield Way commences a mile or so on the further side of the railway, and running a nearly parallel course, joins the upper road at Ivinghoe. These two roads probably result from the original Icknield Way following the broad watershed between the little rivers running east, and the Thames and the Ouse on the west. The modern road, as the country became gradually enclosed, would have its course determined by the convenience of the towns as they came into existence. Many other duplications of the Icknield Way will be met with, each with equal claim to legitimate parentage, since it is impossible for a modern road to touch all the towns and villages on the watershed without intolerable zig-zags. From Beacon Hill the railway and the Icknield Way run side by side to Bledlow Ridge, which is marked by three tumuli and a crosscut in the chalk. From this point the Icknield Way turns towards Saunderton, and follows a road between Princes Risborough and the chalk hills, where a second much larger cross, standing on a triangular base, is cut on the hill-side. These two crosses are accounted for in many ways. They have been said to commemorate a battle with the Danes, again they have been looked upon as the work of the monks of Monks Risborough, who intended them as a guide to travellers, and, more recently still, have been attributed to Cromwell's soldiers. The larger, Whiteleaf Cross, was ordered to be preserved by Act of Parliament in George IV's reign.

On Pulpit Hill, in the grounds of Chequers Court, is a circular camp about a hundred yards in dia-

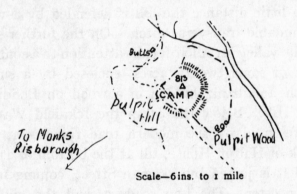

Scale—6 ins. to 1 mile

meter, enclosed by a single bank and ditch, increased to three towards the east. The next spur of hill above Ellesborough, known as Cymbeline's Mount, is adorned with a flagstaff standing on a tumulus, and to the rear are two small enclosures which are stated to be the baileys of a Norman castle. An old tradition exists that two sons of the British chief were slain here when fighting against Aulus Plautius, and support is given to the story from the neighbouring villages of Great and Little Kimble being named " Chine-belles " in early times.   Mr Allcroft in his valuable book " Earthworks of England," says that the mound and banks at Little Kimble are also remains of a Norman castle, perhaps removed there from the fortress on the hill.

From Ellesborough the road runs to Wendover under Bacombe Hill, where the poor remains of a camp can still be traced near the monument to soldiers who fell in the South African War, and at a little distance the hill is defended by a very formidable transverse ditch.   On the further side of the valley Mr Allcroft calls attention to a contour fort of some twenty acres, enclosed by a single ditch and bank, hidden in a wood on Bodding-ton Hill.   Below the camp the Icknield Way is represented by the modern road running at the back of Halton House, till at the bottom of Tring Hill it is joined by Akeman Street, coming from Cirencester.   The two roads ascend the hill to-gether, where Akeman Street passes through Tring, to continue down the valley of the Bulbourne and Eade, whilst the Icknield Way keeping to the west of the town, takes the direction of Pit-stone and Beacon Hills.   Beyond the rifle range, near a group of pit dwellings, Pitstone Hill is crossed by a transverse ditch deep enough to hide a horse and its rider.   Past the tumulus on the ridge, the circle of the beacon is clearly seen, and half - way up the side of the hill is one of those long ledges that so frequently follow the slopes of the downs, and presumably are old pathways. Between Ivinghoe and Dunstable, Cheddington Hill marks the junction of the watershed of the Upper Thames with the Chiltern Hills, and it is here also that the road from Farringdon Ridge would join the Icknield Way, if it was continued through Oxford to Brill and Bolbec. Cheddington Hill is well marked with lynchettes, and to the east on the sides of the road as it mounts the hill to Little Gaddesdon are seen many deep pack-trails as if much traffic had once taken this direction. At the commencement of Dunstable Down, a small valley runs into the chalk, with many tiers of lynchettes on its sides, while a deep and steep cattle-trail ascends the slope of Mount Pleasant to the ridge road on the down above. It may be the remains of an old trail coming over the high ground from the Audreys earthwork, and the camp at St Albans twelve miles away. The Ridgeway after passing two tumuli descends Five Knolls Hill, crosses the Icknield Way, and continues for two miles as a green road along a promontory of the chalk, to the great camp at Totternhoe. By far the greater part of the camp has been destroyed by quarrying, though portions of the banks remain, with a tumulus at their highest point, overlooking the pastures that divide the waters of the Thame and the Ouse. Outside the bank a Roman camp has been constructed by

Totternhoe two additional rectangular banks. The south side
being left undefended except for the steep slope
of the hill above Totternhoe village. About a
mile before coming to the great camp, the green
road passes a single-banked enclosure known as
the Maiden's Bower. Immense quantities of the
bones of oxen have been found within its area,

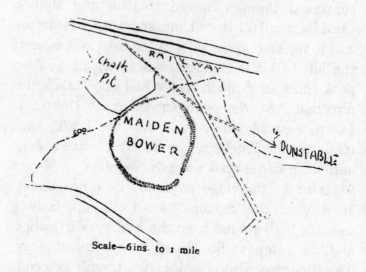

Scale—6 ins. to 1 mile

and to some extent confirm the suggestion that
these secondary camps served as commissariat
depots to the more important fortresses.

The Icknield Way, as traced on the maps from
Five Knolls Hill, runs to Dunstable, where it
crosses Watling Street, then following the road to
Luton, turns at the Half-Way House to Leagrave.
At Wauluds Banks it crosses the little stream that
gives rise to the river Lea, and continues under

TOTTERNHOE CAMP

Warden Hill and Galley Hill, to within a mile of Ravensborough Camp. Sometimes the road is carried right into Luton, where it crosses the river Lea, and following the road to Bedford turns at Grey Ditches to the foot of Galley Hill. Probably neither of these roads are correct. The more likely course,—at least between Totternhoe and Ravensborough Camps,—follows a ridge from the north of the Maiden's Bower to Haughton Regis, crosses the railway at Chalton Cross, and running through the villages of Sundon and Streatley, is carried to the foot of the Barton Hills immediately south of Ravensborough Camp. In addition to being shorter, this line has the advantage of keeping strictly to the watershed, a very important condition when travelling in an undrained country.

Ravens-borough Camp Ravensborough Camp looks out towards Bedford and the valley of the Ouse. It is a large circular enclosure, now surrounded by only a single bank, with a tumulus at the highest point of its circumference. From the camp the Icknield Way follows the county boundary to Telegraph Hill, and from High Down runs as a green road to Punches Corner on the Hitchin and Bedford road, where it joins the modern road to Ickleford. In the village of Pirton, below High Down on the north, is an isolated mound known as Toot Hill. It is surrounded with a ditch, while in a field close by are irregular banks suggesting the remains of an important camp. An alternative route for the

Icknield Way is to follow a track over the western end of High Down to Pirton, and then take the modern road to Ickleford. After passing through the village, the old road crosses the little river Hiz, and then ascends the hill from the railway arch to Willbury Camp. Nearly the whole of the camp

Willbury Camp

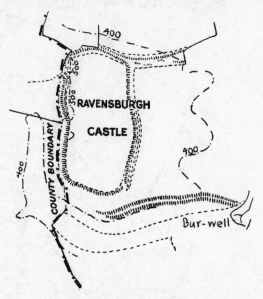

Scale—1 in to 300 yards

has been destroyed by gravel digging, though the bank that remains indicates that it was once of considerable size. If the names "Ickleford" and "Icknieldford" have the same origin, it is clear that the track-way did not avoid the stream at this point, and it was doubtless easier to cross the ford than double back along the watershed by Stevenage, to the south of Hitchin.

The Icknield Way now passes through the Garden City at Letchworth, and follows the railway as far as Baldock. From there the maps clearly show it as keeping to the modern road to Royston, where it crosses the Roman Ermin Street. It is not,

ASHWELL

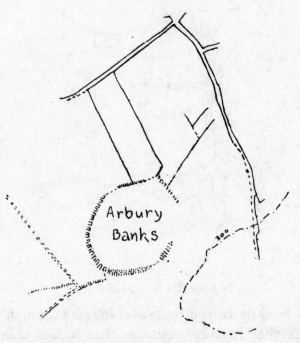

Scale—6 ins. to 1 mile

however, certain that the maps are strictly correct, as by taking the county boundary from Willbury Camp, we come to Arbury Banks, and from there Ashwell Street runs parallel to the Royston road. However, the modern road passes many

tumuli, and beyond Royston these are continued
on the high ground to the left of the Newmarket
road almost as far as Pampisford. A mile and a
half from Royston there is again a choice of routes,
for a green road branches off from the Newmarket
road, and runs, through fields and open country,

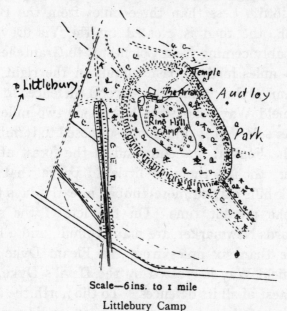

Scale—6 ins. to 1 mile

Littlebury Camp

past Ickleton Grange to Ickleton village, where
the Roman road from Stump Cross again connects
it with the Newmarket road, close to Pampisford
Station. A little south of Ickleton, near Great
Chesterford, is the site of the Roman Station of
Iceanum, and further south again Ring Hill Camp **Littlebury**
stands on the watershed above Littlebury. **Camp**

At Pampisford the Brent Ditch crosses the road,

and is the first of the great dykes that defended the Icknield Way. Coming from the high ground on the south, it ends in the swamps of the Cam and the Granta, and is protected beyond the Granta by the Vandlebury Entrenchments on the Gog Magog Hills, and by a second camp above Shelford. Less than three miles from the Brent Ditch, the road is crossed by the Via Devana, probably coming from Colchester to Grantchester. Two miles further, past tumuli on the right, the Fleam Dyke forms the second defence to the Icknield Way, and stretches about two miles on either side. It is commonly supposed to terminate in the Fens at one end, and in the forest at the other, though there is little to prove that the chalk hills carried more timber in early days than at the present time. On the left of the road, towards Newmarket, are many tumuli, and a little more than six miles from the Fleam Dyke, the Icknield Way is crossed by the Devil's Dyke, the greatest of all its defences. To the north the dyke extends for more than four miles, ending in the Fens on the right bank of the Cam, where it is protected by a camp on higher ground at Burwell. Towards the south it runs for more than two miles to Ditton Green, and in all its course its average height is some sixteen feet above the surface level, while from the bottom of the ditch, which is twenty feet wide, it measures thirty feet in height. Authorities state that it was in the neighbourhood

of the Devil's Dyke that the Romans, under
Ostorius, defeated the Icenians. Tacitus says that
" The Britons, enclosed by their own fortifications,

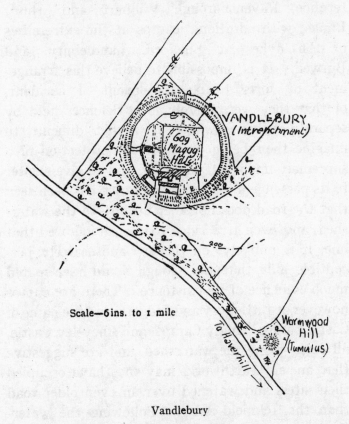

Scale—6 ins. to 1 mile

Vandlebury

and pressed on every side, were thrown into the
utmost confusion. Yet, even in that distress,
conscious of the guilt of rebellion, and seeing no
way of escape, they fought to the last and gave
signal proofs of heroic bravery."

In the course of the Icknield Way, north of the Thames, camps have already been passed on Pulpit Hill, at Wendover, Boddington, Totternhoe, Ravensborough, Willbury, and Arbury Banks, with additional camps at the extremities of the dykes at Shelford, Vandlebury, and Burwell. It is impossible to believe this arrangement of forts to be the result of accident, or that they were merely local defences held by separate tribes; whilst it is not difficult to imagine their being built for the protection of a supremely important highway, and to give shelter to its passengers. From Ickleford it has been seen that the road does not keep strictly to the watershed, and even if a ridge road once followed that line, it is unlikely, on the low and scarcely perceptible hills, that the plough would have spared much evidence of its existence. There are camps however at Littlebury and Lidgate, and the name of Castle Camps, Shudy Camps, and Cheveley Castle, all occur along the watershed, and are suggestive that ancient earthworks may once have occupied their sites, and watched over an even older road than the Icknield Way. Following the watershed, we come to War Banks, and Bun's Banks, which are said to be the remains of prehistoric earthworks, and five miles east of Castle Acre there are also remains of old earthworks. The watershed then runs parallel to the Pedlar's Way, and turning to the so-called Danish entrench-

ments at South Creak, takes the direction of South Creak Camp
Crab's Castle—now destroyed—and finally leads
to the ancient port of Wells.

After crossing the Kennett at Kentford, the
Icknield Way turns north from the Bury St
Edmunds road near two tumuli. A little beyond
the angle thus formed the Black Ditch extends
for two miles, parallel to the road to Bury St
Edmunds facing Barrow Fields. It is generally supposed to belong to the defences of the
Icknield Way, which at one time it may have
crossed, as it is by no means certain that the
exact position of the track-way has been preserved. Beyond the Black Ditch, the Icknield
Way soon divides into two branches, one crossing the little river Lark at Icklingham, the
other at Lackford. Or following the line of the
modern road, the crossing might equally well
have taken place at Mildenhall. In any case the
ancient highway does not here avoid the river, as
it might have done, by rounding the Linnet and
the Lark, to the east of Bury St Edmunds. The
reason may be that there is no boggy approach
to the river ; the bed is firm and sandy, giving
good footing to horses and cattle, whilst, along
the watershed, the spongy land must have been
negotiated that gives rise to the Waveney and
Little Ouse. It is singular to find the Wiltshire
names " Kennett " and " Mildenhall " repeated
at so great a distance, whilst "Ashley" close

by, is a name that occurs wherever green roads can be followed.

With three alternative crossings of the Lark, it is difficult to determine the course taken by the Icknield Way across the sandy heaths of Norfolk. It is generally supposed to follow the Pilgrim's Way from Icklingham to Thetford, and thence by Green Lane to Roudham Heath. Here Mr W. G. Clark considers that three main branches were given off, one going east to Norfolk, the second north to Castle Acre, and the third to Hockwold. The last stands on the edge of the Fens, once a great inland sea giving an all too easy access for strangers to penetrate into the land. A mile to the north of this third branch,—after it has crossed Stoke Ferry,—are found the celebrated Grim's Graves, which Canon Greenwell has taught the world were once a flint ordnance factory. The Norman Castles at Thetford and Castle Acre are believed to occupy the sites of old contour forts, and the numerous finds of flint instruments in the neighbourhood of Thetford, point to its having been a populous centre in prehistoric times. The great Motte, still in good preservation within the earthwork, is certainly Norman, and the largest perhaps to be found in the country. At Castle Acre, both the situation and the line of outer ramparts are very suggestive of a large and important early earthwork. Here the motte occupies just such a position as many tumuli in the older camps, with the addition of an inner ditch which cuts it off from the rest of the enclosure. Running parallel to the Icknield Way, between Thetford and Castle Acre, the Devil's Dyke extends for a good ten miles along the edge of the Fens, and may have served as a possible defence against enemies from the sea. It stretches north from the road to Hockwold as far as the river Wissey, and after a break of four miles is again traced from Caldicot to the river Nar, at Narborough, where there are remains of a British village. The Icknield Way continues north from Castle Acre, terminating either at Castle Rising, where the sea once came much nearer to the site of the present Norman castle, or possibly followed the course of the Pilgrim's Way to Brancaster, which in later days became the headquarters of the Counts of the Saxon shore.

CHAPTER X

THE WATERSHED OF THE UPPER THAMES

" That which you call the spirit of the ages past,
    Is but, in truth, the spirit of some few authors,
    In which these ages are beheld reflected,
    With what distortion strange, heaven only knows."

ON a northern spur of Avebury Plateau
the partially destroyed camp of Bincknol
looks out over the watershed of the
Thames and Bristol Avon, with Ringsbury Camp
six miles away standing on the highest ground.
Along the watershed lie the villages of Lydiard
Green, Lydiard Millicent, and Lydiard Tregoze,
the origin of their name being probably the same
as Lid, Lad, and Lun, meaning popular or frequented, and suggesting that the watershed was
once a busy highway. It is directly in the line
of route to the north from Fosbury, following the
watershed of the Kennett and the Salisbury Avon,
which we have already seen is the only opportunity
of making the journey north from the south of
England, without having to compass the sodden
clay of the Thames Valley. It is through
Ringsbury that communication would have been
made from the great centre of Avebury with the
Cotswold Hills, and the country north of the

Ringsbury
Camp

Thames Basin. The camp must have received further importance from the traffic passing east and west along the Farringdon Ridge, and offering the shortest route from Avebury to the Chiltern Hills. As already mentioned, it stands behind the little Jacobean house at Restrop, with a beautiful view westward. The banks and ditch are well preserved, and on the neighbouring Paven Hill, are further remains of extensive earthworks. A little more than two miles distant on Bury Hill, is a bank and ditch forming the segment of a camp now almost destroyed, and which may well have served as a supply camp to Ringsbury.

The watershed from Ringsbury circles round the Swill Brook to Trewsbury Camp, two miles from Cirencester, situated immediately above the springs that form the source of the Thames. The centre of the camp is now occupied by a private house, and the vallum partly encloses the surrounding lawns, while the side of the hill sloping to the Thames and Severn Canal now makes a delightful terraced garden, and completes the defence of the camp. It is at present so well cared for, that it seems a little ungracious to fear any further injury, though the spade of the gardener can be almost as destructive as the plough. A home enclosed in an ancient place of safety, should add so much to the pleasure of its possession, that there ought to be no risk of its banks ever being destroyed.

North of Trewsbury the watershed runs through

Trewsbury Camp

a high and open tableland, between a little branch of the river Churn and the village of Miserdon, near the sources of the Stroud Water. The land is full of many tumuli, long barrows, and earthworks, as at Minchinhampton, Woodchester, and **Kimsbury Camp** Owlpen, whilst west and north of Stroud Water, nearly every promontory and outlying hill is

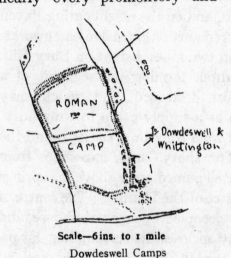

ROMAN
700
CAMP

To Dowdeswell & Whittington

Scale—6 ins. to 1 mile
Dowdeswell Camps

defended by its camp. The most important are Kimsbury, where much quarrying has been done, and the camp near C r a n h a m, which, judging from the extended area of its remains,

must once have been of considerable size. It is hidden in a wood at the top of a hill, but its ramparts are in places now smoothed out almost beyond recognition, though here and there supported by a stone wall. Above Miserdon the watershed follows the high road to Birdlip, almost 1000 feet high, and continuing along the high ground, passes a camp with a **Hartley Hill Camp** single bank on Crickley Hill, to reach Hartley Hill Camp overlooking Cheltenham, which is also,

KIMSBURY CAMP

in much danger from quarrying. From Hartley Hill the high land turns due west to Dowdeswell, and separates the river Churn,—flowing to the Thames,—from the Chelt, a little tributary of the Severn. The situation at the angle of the hills at

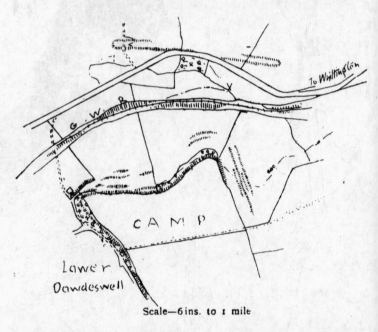

Scale—6 ins. to 1 mile

Dowdeswell Camp Dowdeswell must have been of great military importance, for in addition to the earlier earthwork of which little remains, two large Roman camps are placed on the slopes of the Hill, their banks being still clear and distinct. The hills now again turn north, rising to 1070 feet, and sheltering Cheltenham from the east. A beautiful green road follows the high ground to Cleeve Common, and at the highest point of the hills there are two small camps and several tumuli. Outlying hills extend into the Severn Valley, with camps on their summits at Nottingham Hill, Langley Hill, Oxenton Hill, and Dixton. The great number of camps on the spurs of the Cotswolds overlooking the Severn, between

Cleeve Hill

Stroud and Cheltenham, must have served some special purpose, possibly as defence against danger from the river, or perhaps raids from beyond the river. Whatever the danger, it appears to have lasted into Roman times, and may account for their great camps at Dowdeswell. From Cleeve the hills turn east to Roel Gate, where there is a circular camp with a single bank, and at this point the watershed again bends north and encloses the

Winchcombe Valley. A little to the north of
Winchcombe, at Hailes, there are two small circular
camps, that, as now seen, appear to have been of
only secondary importance. Following the hills
from Hailes, a green road passes Toddington on
Shunbarrow its way to Snowshill, leaving the camp at Shun-
Camp barrow Hill a little to the left. The camp is not
placed on the extreme point of this shoulder of
the Cotswolds, but on the slopes looking south,
towards Nottingham, Langley and Oxenton Hills.
A small farm-house stands within the ramparts
on the northern face, and a fairly perfect circular
bank and ditch complete the enclosure. There
are suggestions of additional ramparts without,
and the steep sides of a natural gully, that runs
round the face of the hill, must have made the
position of considerable strength.

The green road now skirts the edge of the hills
from Snowshill, past the tower above Broadway, as
Farncombe far as Farncombe. This bold headland overlooks
Camp the Vale of Evesham, and was evidently the site
of a considerable camp. It is now partly occupied
by the buildings of Happy Land Farm, but lengths
of banks and ditches clearly indicate a circular
enclosure of great size, whilst certain suggestive
undulations in the surrounding land, and a double
tier of ramparts on the hill-side, can only be the
remains of a fortress of very unusual dimensions.
Meon Hill A ridge stretching north to Meon Hill is defended
by a long length of earthwork, and at its termina-

MEON HILL AND CAMP

tion a large area of the summit of the hill is enclosed by a powerful foss and rampart.   On a neighbouring hill above Illington there is a small Roman camp, as if placed as an observation post to watch the doings on Meon Hill.

From Farncombe the Thames watershed turns sharply to the east, giving rise to the head-waters of the Stour branch of Shakespeare's Avon.   It keeps almost exactly along the line of the excellent road known as the Five Mile Drove, leading through Bourton-on-the-Hill to Moreton-in-the-Marsh.   On entering Moreton there is a short length of bank on the opposite side of the road to the cricket ground, which is all that remains of what appears to have been a rectangular camp.

Although   Moreton-in-the-Marsh lies on the lowest part of the Thames watershed, it is still high enough to divide the waters of Warwickshire from the sources of the Evenlode, and the dividing line is fairly marked by the road to Chastleton, that passes the Four Shires Stone.   The Manor House of Chastleton is one of the best specimens of seventeenth century building in the country, and is associated with interesting historical incidents.   On the hill above is a small but singularly well-preserved circular camp, where, as it occupies a very commanding position, a much larger earthwork might have been expected.   But there is no knowing how much has been destroyed, and it is perhaps surprising that any portion of

Chastleton

the camp should have survived the changes of so
many centuries.

The little road from the camp joins the Ridgeway, along the high bastion of hills that enclose
the basin of the Thames. The metalling of
the road is often but a narrow strip, and frequently out of repair, but its broad turf margins
are proof of its former importance, and its position
along the hill-tops is a certificate of age as old as
the first rude efforts of our civilization. Some
three miles to the east a small group of pine trees
on the right mark the position of Rollright Stones, Rollright
a small stone circle built on the same general plan
as Avebury and Stonehenge. If, as Stukeley says,
Stonehenge compared to Avebury was " as a
parish church to a cathedral " Rollright can hardly
aspire to greater dignity than a Little Bethel,
though from the weathering of the stones, and
their untrimmed shape, it may be as old as Avebury itself. The stones average three to four feet
high, and are now placed close together, and protected by an iron railing. This can hardly have been
their original position, as Stukeley says that in 1719,
the circle was thirty-five yards in diameter, and
gives an illustration showing considerable spaces
between the stones, while he states that the
villagers had removed many for building houses
and bridges. In a field on the opposite side of the
road, the King Stone, some seven feet high, points
to the rising sun and occupies the same relative

position to the circle as the Pointer Stone at Stonehenge. One or two round barrows, with the long barrow beyond the King Stone, and the cromlech to the east of the circle, still exist, though most of the barrows and other earthworks mentioned by Stukeley have disappeared. There is an old tradition that the circle represents a King and his army turned to stone by a witch, and the cromlech a group of whispering Knights who conspired against their King.

Tadmarton Camps The Ridgeway closely follows the watershed over Oatley Hill, and gives a wide and splendid outlook both to the north and south. On the broad level plateau of Tadmarton Hill, there are two large camps enclosed by single banks, one filled with gorse, bracken, and brushwood, while the surface of the other is smooth and level turf. The situation of the hill at the angle of the watershed, and the natural strength of the position, raises expectation of more important earthworks than these two camps, and it would be interesting, when the crops are carried, to examine the slopes of the hill for such remains. From Tadmarton the watershed turns north, leaving the camp on Madmarston Hill on the right, and following the Ridgeway above Compton Wyniates, runs along Edge Hill to the site of a camp at Knowle End. Little of the camp is left, but from the segment of the rampart that remains, it appears to have enclosured two or three acres. From Edge Hill

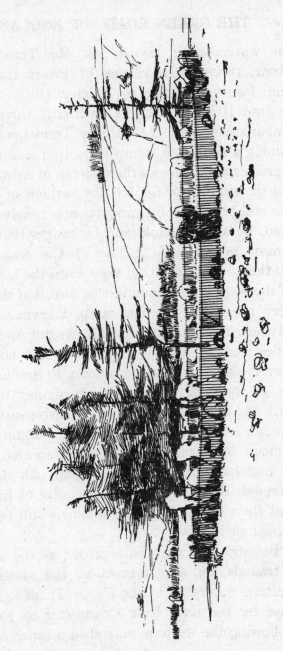

ROLLRIGHT STONES

the watershed is traced past the Three Shires Stone, through the villages of Priors Hardwick, and Priors Marston, to Arbury Hill. A little beyond Hellidon a bridle path cuts through the embankment over the Catesby Tunnel, and after joining a field path from Charwelton, continues as a green road to the southern slopes of Arbury Hill. On the summit of the hill the outlines of a camp can still be traced, by ramparts now nearly obliterated, by a steep bank, and by hedges that follow almost accurately the line of the escarpment. To the east is a beautiful view down the full length of the Nene Valley, and in this direction there is a very interesting Roman camp, known as Castle Ditches, that stands on high ground about two miles west of Watling Street. To the north the view is shut in by a ridge running to Borough Hill, an off-shoot of the watershed, similar to Meon Hill, and also occupied by an extensive earthwork, though from the presence of farm buildings, it is difficult to trace its banks as a connected whole. A popular belief exists that an oak tree on Borough Hill marks the exact centre of England, and there young men and maidens still resort to record their vows.

Borough Hill may be regarded as the apex of a triangle, its sides formed by the eastern and western watershed of the Upper Thames, and its base by the river from Cirencester to Reading. Following the western watershed a series of great

[margin note: Arbury Hill Camp]

[margin note: Borough Hill Camp]

camps have been passed from Avebury to Bincknol, Ringsbury, Trewsbury, Kimsbury, Cranham, Hartley Hill, Cleeve, Dowdeswell, Roel Gate,

Cattle Track to Borough Hill Camp

Hailes, Shunbarrow, Farncombe, Chastleton, Tadmarton, Madmarston, Knowle Hill and Arbury Hill. On the eastern watershed there are earthworks at Thenford, Rainsborough, Beaumont, and Bolbec, where the line of camps along the Chiltern

Hills are taken up. As the hills are much lower along the eastern than the western side of the Thames basin, it is probable that agriculture has destroyed many of the old forts, and certain that it has greatly injured those that remain. The Romans also constructed their great roads along much the same course as these earlier lines of communication: the Foss Way follows the western side of the triangle, and Watling Street the eastern, their base being formed by Akeman Street following the Thames along its northern bank from Cirencester to Tring.

Arbury Hill marks the northern turning-point of the watershed, and from here it may be traced south to Canons Ashby and Culworth, where it follows the line of Banbury Lane to Thenford Hill. On the hill a mere fragment of bank remains, but it appears to have been part of an earthwork that once enclosed the whole plateau. The situation is exactly such as was usually chosen for the old contour forts, and besides the trails along the watershed, Banbury Lane keeps it in direct communication with Hunsbury Camp, near Northampton.

Rains-borough Camp   Continuing south through Hinton-in-the-Hedges, two miles from Brackley, the watershed reaches Rainsborough Camp, a good-sized circular enclosure, though surrounded by only a single bank and ditch, now planted with beech trees. From Rainsborough the watershed passes

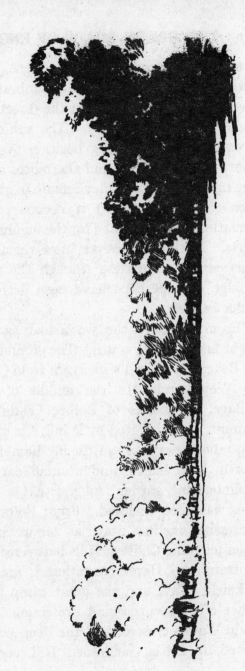

RAINSBOROUGH CAMP

a small camp concealed by a copse, in the angle formed by the Brackley and Banbury roads, and then still continues west in the direction of Beaumont Castle at Mixbury. The site of this castle occupies a commanding position overlooking the sources of the Ouse, and the motte and banks of the inner and outer bailey remain in good preservation. As at Thenford it occupies just such a situation as was selected for the building of contour forts. Nothing, however, now remains to prove this earlier occupation, though the name of the village may perhaps have been derived from an older earthwork.

Mixbury

From Mixbury the watershed again turns at right angles to the south. The ground falls rapidly to Beacon Hill, and rises again from Quainton Hill to Whitchurch. In the middle of Whitchurch village, the banks of Bolbec Castle occupy the summit of an isolated little hill, the camp measuring about seventy yards in diameter. To the north, high banks, and a small earthwork in a neighbouring garden, suggest that a much larger area was once enclosed. From Bolbec Castle the watershed inclines north as far as Stewkley, and then joins the Chiltern Hills between Ivinghoe and Totternhoe. Here connection is made with the Icknield Way, and the great camp at the latter place offers security and protection. If the Icknield Way is crossed, and the deep pack-trails followed up Little Gaddesden Hill, communication

Bolbec Castle

could be made by the Audreys, with the camp at St Albans, and possibly London. Or again, travellers from Norfolk, instead of crossing the Thames at Streatley, could, if the river was in flood and impassable, turn off by the alternative route round the Thames watershed to Avebury, and finally reach the English Channel by way of Camelot, without having to cross a single river throughout the entire length of their journey.

Besides the camps surrounding the basin of the Thames, it will be seen that there are others situated on the watersheds between the little rivers Churn, Windrush, Evenlode, and Cherwell. Some of these earthworks may have served as cattle compounds, though Mangersbury appears to have been a great and powerful stronghold. The trackways connecting these forts with the outer ring must have kept open the communications of the country, whilst the camps would have helped to preserve peace and to support authority.

L'ENVOI

The title of my book is I fear more appropriate to its promise than its performance, but short week-ends snatched from other duties, have not allowed me time to examine the more distant watersheds. If I can induce others to take their walks along these ancient paths, and to communicate the result of their researches to the Hon. Sec. of the Society of Green Roads, Lincoln's Inn Court, Lincoln's Inn Fields, London, W.C., it may be possible in the future, to give a fuller account of the Green Roads of England.

INDEX

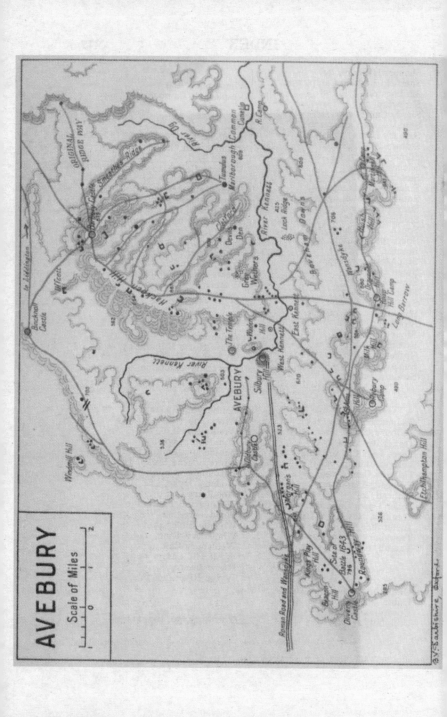

AVEBURY

Scale of Miles

0   1   2

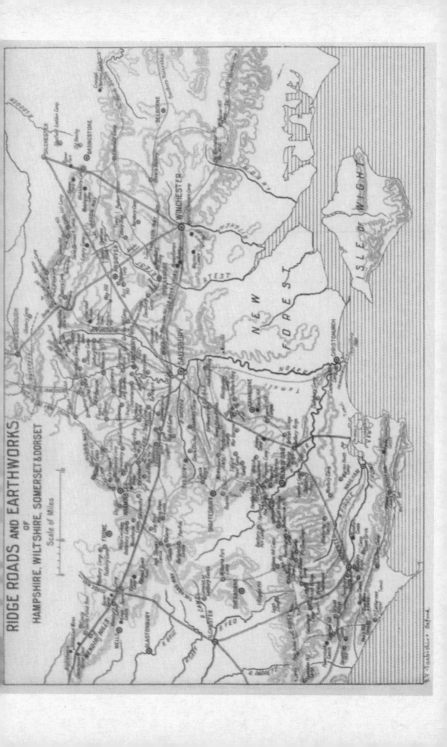

THE PASSAGE OF THE SEVERN FROM THE MENDIPS TO WALES

B.V.Darbishire, Oxford.

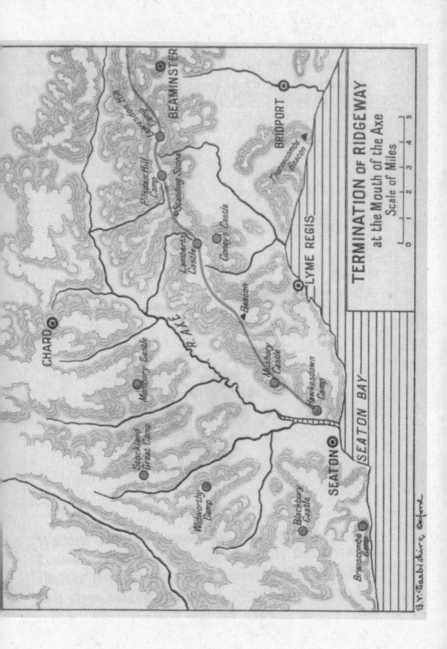

TERMINATION of RIDGEWAY
at the Mouth of the Axe

Scale of Miles

0 1 2 3 4 5

B.Y. Tanbishire, Oxford

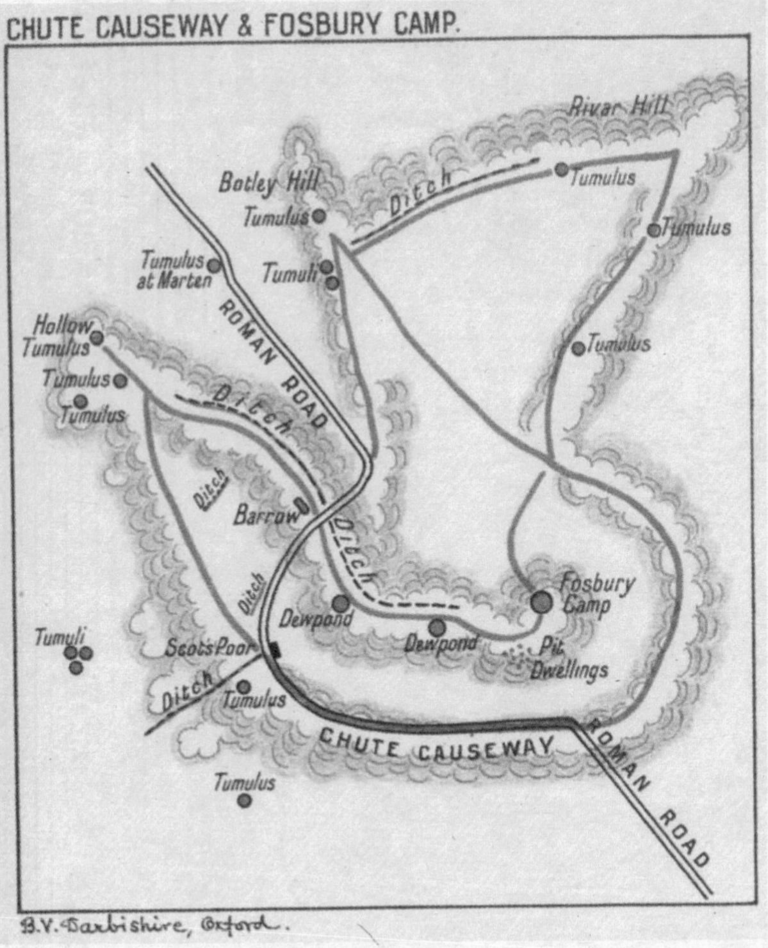

CHUTE CAUSEWAY & FOSBURY CAMP.

River Hill
Botley Hill
Tumulus
Ditch
Tumulus
Tumulus
Tumulus
at Marten
Tumuli
ROMAN ROAD
Hollow
Tumulus
Tumulus
Ditch
Tumulus
Tumulus
Ditch
Ditch
Barrow
Ditch
Fosbury
Camp
Dewpond
Tumuli
Scots Poor
Dewpond
Pit
Dwellings
Ditch
Tumulus
CHUTE CAUSEWAY
ROMAN ROAD
Tumulus

B.V. Darbishire, Oxford.

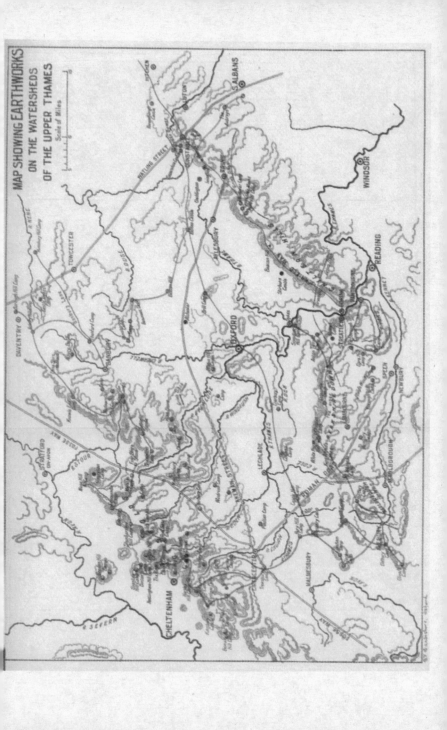

MAP SHOWING EARTHWORKS
ON THE WATERSHEDS
OF THE UPPER THAMES

Scale of Miles

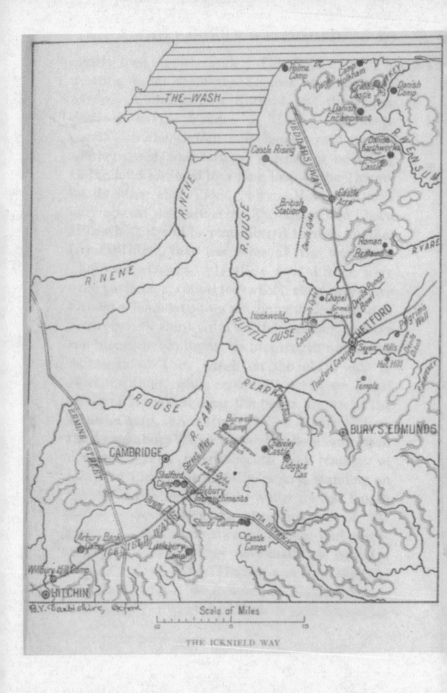

THE WASH

R. NENE
R. NENE
R. OUSE
R. OUSE

Holme Camp
Danish Camp
Holkham
Cross Castle
Danish Camp
Danish Encampment
Castle Rising
Danish Earthworks
Castle
British Station
Castle Acre
Roman Remains
R. YARE
R. OUSE
Devil's Dyke
R. LITTLE OUSE
Hockwold
Chapel
Grimes Graves
Devil's Punch Bowl
Castle
THETFORD
Pilgrim's Well
Seven Hills
Thetford Castle
Hoit Hill
Temple
R. LARK
ERMINE STREET
R. CAM
R. OUSE
Burwell Camp
Devil's Dyke
CAMBRIDGE
Street Way
Shelford Camp
Pampisbury Encampments
Fleam Dyke
Chevley Castle
Lidgate Cas
BURY S. EDMUNDS
VIA DEVANA
Shudy Camps
Castle Camps
Arbury Banks
Litlebury Camp
ICKNIELD WAY
Wilbury Hill Camp
HITCHIN

R.V. Darbishire, Oxford

Scale of Miles

THE ICKNIELD WAY